BEYOND EDUCATIONAL REFORM

Bringing Teachers Back In

EDITED BY

**Andy Hargreaves
and Roy Evans**

OPEN UNIVERSITY PRESS

Buckingham • Philadelphia

Open University Press
Celtic Court
22 Ballmoor
Buckingham
MK18 1XW

and
1900 Frost Road, Suite 101
Bristol, PA 19007, USA

First Published 1997

A catalogue record of this book is available from the British Library

ISBN   0 335 19995 X (pb)   0 335 19996 8 (hb)

Library of Congress Cataloging-in-Publication Data
Beyond educational reform / edited by Andy Hargreaves and Roy
Evans.
        p. cm.
    Includes bibliographical references and index.
    ISBN 0-335-19996-8 (hc). — ISBN 0-335-19995-X (pbk.)
    1. Teacher participation in administration. 2. Educational
change. I. Hargreaves, Andy. II. Evans, Roy.
LB2806.45.B48 1997
371.2—dc21   97–12932
                                                              CIP

Typeset by Graphicraft Typesetters Ltd, Hong Kong
Printed in Great Britain

BEYOND
EDUCATIONAL
REFORM

Bringing Teachers Back In

CONTENTS

NOTES ON CONTRIBUTORS

Brian J. Caldwell is Professor and Head, Department of Education Policy and Management at the University of Melbourne, Australia. His main interests lie in the areas of policy, leadership, resource allocation and the management of change, especially in public education where significant responsibility, authority and accountability are decentralized to schools. He is co-author with Jim Spinks of *The Self-Managing School* (Falmer 1988), *Leading the Self-Managing School* (Falmer 1992) and *Beyond the Self-Managing School* (Falmer 1998). In a rare academic–ministerial writing partnership, he wrote *The Future of Schools: Lessons from the Reform of Public Education* (Falmer 1998) with co-author Don Hayward, who served as Minister for Education in Victoria from 1992 to 1996. He has worked extensively in the international arena with invited presentations and consultancies in fifteen nations, including assignments with the Asia Development Bank, OECD, UNESCO, and World Bank.

Christopher Day is Professor of Education, Director of Research and Co-director of the Centre for Teacher and School Development in the School of Education and Head of Advanced Studies, University of Nottingham. Prior to this he worked as a teacher, lecturer and local education authority adviser. His particular concerns centre upon the continuing professional development of teachers, teachers' thinking, leadership and school cultures. Recent publications include *Insights into Teachers' Thinking and Action* (co-edited with M. Pope and P. Denicolo; Falmer Press 1990), *Research on Teacher Thinking: Towards Understanding Professional Development* (co-edited with J. Calderhead and P. Denicolo; Falmer Press 1993), co-author of *Leading Primary Schools* (Paul Chapman Ltd 1998), and editor of a series for Open University Press entitled *Developing Teachers and Teaching* (current). He is Editor of *Teachers and Teaching: Theory and Practice*, an international journal; and co-editor of the *International Journal of Educational Action Research* (EARJ).

Roy Evans was previously Assistant Dean responsible for research in the Faculty of Education at Roehampton Institute, London, and Director of the Centre for Educational Development and Research (CEDARR). He has written and researched extensively on professional issues connected with the provision of effective education for children with special needs, and is a past President of the National Association for Remedial Education. As Chief Editor of the international journal *Early Child Development and Care* for the past 18 years, he has been involved with international efforts to improve the professionalism of early childhood teachers in different cultures. A recent book with Olivia Saracho (*Teacher Preparation for Early Childhood Education*) addresses key issues for initial training and continuing professional development, with particular emphasis on how appropriate and legitimate teacher knowledge is identified.

Ivor Goodson is a Professor in the Centre for Applied Research in Education at the University of East Anglia. He is also the Frederica Warner Scholar at the Margaret Warner Graduate School of Education and Human Development, University of Rochester. He is the author of a range of books on curriculum and life history studies. They include *School Subjects and Curriculum Change, Biography, Identity and Schooling* (with Rob Walker) and *Studying Teachers' Lives*. He is the Founding Editor and North American Editor of the *Journal of Education Policy* and the National Editor of *Qualitative Studies in Education*.

Andy Hargreaves is Director of the International Centre for Educational Change and Professor of Educational Administration at the Ontario Institute for Studies in Canada and also International Research Professor of the Roehampton Institute, London. He has written and researched widely on teachers' work, teacher cultures and professional development in Europe and North America. Among his recent books are *Changing Teachers, Changing Times* (Cassell, Teachers' College Press and OISE Press 1994) which received the 1995 Outstanding Writing Award from the American Association of Colleges for Teacher Education; *Schooling for Change* (with Lorna Earl and James Ryan; Falmer Press 1996); and *What's Worth Fighting For? Working Together for Your School*, second edition (with Michael Fullan; Ontario Public School Teachers' Federation, Open University Press and Teachers College Press 1996).

Gary McCulloch is Professor of Education at the University of Sheffield. His recent published work includes *Educational Reconstruction: the 1944 Education Act and the 21st Century* (Woburn 1994). His current research is on the social history of mass secondary education and on the professional cultures of teaching.

Milbrey W. McLaughlin is Professor of Education and Public Policy at Stanford University. She is Co-director (with Joan Talbert) of the Center for Research on the Contexts of Teaching, and co-principal investigator (with Shirley Brice Heath) of a multi-year project that examines community-based resources for youth in diverse community settings. McLaughlin also directs and co-chairs the Pew Forum on Educational Reform. She is the author or co-author of several books and articles on education policy issues, contexts for teaching and learning, productive environments for youth, and community-based organizations. Her recent books include: *Teacher Learning: New Policies, New Practices* (with Ida Oberman; Teachers

College Press 1996) *Urban Sanctuaries* (with Merita A. Irby and Juliet Langman; Jossey-Bass 1994); *Identity and Inner-City Youth: Beyond Ethnicity and Gender* (with Shirley Brice Heath; Teachers College Press 1993); *Teaching for Understanding: Challenges for Policy and Practice* (with David K. Cohen and Joan E. Talbert; Jossey-Bass 1993); and *Teachers' Work* (with Judith Warren Little; Teachers College Press 1993).

N. Ken Shimahara is Professor of Anthropology of Education in the Graduate School of Education, Rutgers University. Among his many publications are *Learning to Teach in Two Cultures: Japan and the United States* (with Akira Sakai; Garland Publishing 1995) and *Teacher Education in Industrialized Nations* (edited with I. Holowinsky; Garland Publishing 1995).

1 TEACHERS AND EDUCATIONAL REFORM

Andy Hargreaves
and Roy Evans

Teachers' responses to educational reform

Educational reform in England and Wales has gone through many turbulent years since the 1988 Education Reform Act, which brought sweeping changes to the structures and processes of state schooling. No one is more aware of the turbulence of these reforms than the teachers who have had to implement them. There is as yet no consistent view about how 'effective' these reforms have been in transforming teachers' practice. Reluctant rather than enthusiastic compliance among teachers has been one widely reported pattern of response (e.g. Helsby and McCulloch 1996). For many teachers who have reacted in this way, the National Curriculum and other related reforms have created senses of loss, even bereavement, as purposes that teachers value highly such as their relationships with their pupils, and their pupils' broader personal and social development, have been crowded out and cast aside by a narrowly conceived and onerous set of content demands (Nias 1989; Best 1994).

Other studies have pointed to the stubbornly creative capacity of many teachers to resist the dictates of National Curriculum reforms and to redefine the reforms to suit their own purposes (e.g. Ball and Bowe 1992). Nor are these exceptions confined to one or two individual schools. Capitulation to Conservative educational reforms has not been universal; beleaguered as they have become, several local education authorities have made spirited efforts to develop their own unique brands of educational reform. The system-wide commitment to supportive school improvement and professional learning for teachers in Birmingham Education Authority under its innovative director, Tim Brighouse, is one of the most visible and courageous exemplars of this pattern. But valuable as they are, these local variations in educational reform have not nullified the overall national pattern, whose effects remain pervasive. Our concern in this opening chapter is, in this sense, not with *all* educational changes and reforms, but with the impact on teachers of nationally generated and imposed ones.

A third set of analyses points to unintended consequences of national reforms on curriculum and assessment that may actually be beneficial for teachers and teaching. Teachers' sophistication in assessment expertise is one such consequence; and improvements in the amount and depth of professional collaboration among primary teachers as they have been compelled to coordinate their curriculum throughout the school more thoroughly, are another (Woods 1993; D. Hargreaves 1995).

These differing accounts of the effects of educational reform upon teachers in England and Wales may vary because they focus on different groups of teachers, or different aspects of their work. They may also vary because of the value stand-points and research orientations of their respective authors – some preferring to criticize the foundational shift in educational policy frameworks, while others choose to celebrate the capacity of individual teachers to resist and circumvent, and even prosper from, these foundational changes. Whatever their differences, all researchers concur that the effects of educational reforms on teachers in England and Wales in terms of the reforms' substance, scope and speed of implementation have been devastatingly exhausting. And the most serious effects have often been on the most committed teachers, who have been 'crippled by conscientiousness' as they have tried to work miracles and to make profoundly unreasonable reforms work with the children they care for in their classes (Campbell and Neill 1994).

It is in this context that some recent critiques from senior educational policymakers about the low quality of professionalism among the nation's teachers have proved particularly galling – adding insult to injury for a consistently beleaguered teaching force. Equally problematic is the way that positive interest in and support for processes of school improvement have become rapidly side-tracked into politically fuelled moral panics about 'failing' teachers in 'failing' schools and the need to 'turn them around'. In the aftermath of legislative educational reform and its impact, even these efforts to engage teachers in reform and to address school-level change processes, remain locked within policy discourses of failure and blame – discourses with which many senior educational researchers have been oddly complicit.

In this opening chapter, we want to look at how this post-Reform Act discourse within policy and research is continuing to present teachers' work, teachers' cultures and teachers' professionalism in a negative light. We want to draw attention to reform discourses in other countries that represent the role that teachers can and should play in educational change in very different ways. Then we want to explore alternative agendas for educational reform in Britain that might capitalize effectively on, rather than castigate and dismiss, the efforts and energies of the teaching force. Finally, we will introduce the chapters within this book that address the relationship between teachers, educational reform and educational research in Britain and beyond.

Teachers as anti-intellectuals

One of the key interventions in the approach to educational reform that is coming to characterize the post-Reform Act era was a significant speech to the Royal Society of Arts by the Office for Standards in Education's (Ofsted) Chief Inspector Chris Woodhead (Woodhead 1995). This began promisingly by reminding the audience that legislation only sets a framework for improvement; it is teachers who must make that improvement happen. This makes eminent sense. Teachers are indeed the indispensable agents of educational change (Fullan and Hargreaves 1996). Where educational change is concerned, if a teacher can't or won't do it, it simply can't be done.

There is well-established and increasing evidence that the quality of teaching and learning inside the classroom is shaped by the quality of relationships teachers have with their colleagues outside the classroom (Rosenholtz 1989). Good teachers are also good learners. Better learning among pupils in classrooms comes about when there are strong professional cultures of teaching in staffrooms. So to say that we must include teachers in change and help strengthen the cultures that bind them to their colleagues is not to be romantic or sentimental about teachers; it is to face up to the realities of teaching and how teachers change for the better.

Notwithstanding some forced collaboration among teachers that has been brought about by the necessity of implementing National Curriculum requirements, the Conservative educational reforms in England and Wales have done little to build professional cultures of teaching. The reforms have generally pandered to high-profile parents, diverted teachers' energies to public relations and paperwork, weighed teachers down with interminable testing requirements and overloads of content, and caused a rush for early retirement. In the face of a non-consultative and over-centralized bureaucracy, teachers eventually rose up together, refused to comply with testing requirements, and said 'enough'. Government had overreached itself and had helped demolish exactly those professional cultures of teaching on which the whole reform edifice should have been built.

The investigation into and final report on National Curriculum implementation coordinated by Sir Ron Dearing eventually pulled Government back from the abyss and started to restore some respect for the teaching profession. And for a brief moment, early in his speech, when he spoke of the need to move beyond legislative frameworks and to attend to the professional culture of teaching, it looked as if the Chief Inspector might extend this understanding still further. But this was not to be.

Mr Woodhead (1995) complained that the culture of teaching was not 'charac-terized by a sense of intellectual adventure, by an enthusiasm for critical reflection on ideas, values, assumptions, current practices, by a refusal to allow the working hypothesis to harden into the unexamined orthodoxy'. Teachers, he said, were subject to 'unquestioning and ultimately irrational commitments'. What was needed was a more questioning culture among school staffs, where teachers would reflect on their beliefs and practices in a process of continuous review.

Yet imposing change from on high has never been a good starting point for intellectual adventure. Excessive stress, loss of control and mechanical obedience provide no proper foundation for risk-taking, yet these have been the very effects of legislated educational reform in England and Wales (Cooper 1994). Furthermore, some of the major stimuli for intellectual investigation among teachers – university schools of education – have been the subject of relentless attacks from Government. By making anything and everything school-based, and pitting schools competitively against each other in a market scramble for parental customers, teachers have been largely confined to their own schools, shielded from precisely that professional learning which could provide the kind of questioning Mr Woodhead wants.

The previous Government's record of reform has been a poor starting point for raising standards of intellectual questioning among teachers. It has been a horrible example of all that Woodhead criticizes. Woodhead's tone of moral opprobrium concerning teachers has only made matters worse. Of course, pious injunctions for teachers to pull their socks up are familiar fare in educational reform. However, strong professional cultures cannot be bullied into existence: it takes care and commitment over many years, along with active trust in the autonomy and integrity of each individual who belongs to those cultures, to secure their collective development over time (A. Hargreaves 1994; Talbert and McLaughlin 1994). Had the previous Government ever been serious about sponsoring teaching as 'intellectual adventure', it would have supported grass-roots movements of teacher development and inquiry such as teacher research and action research, for which a few brave communities of British teachers and teacher educators have become renowned the world over (e.g. Elliott 1991).

Professional cultures of teaching are also built on emotional as well as intellectual strength. In some ways, such cultures are quite proudly non-rational. Care, for example, is a big part of teachers' commitment. It is what brings most primary teachers (most of whom are also women) into teaching and keeps them there (Nias 1989; Acker 1995). Emotional connectedness, moral support, reciprocal help and mutual trust in pursuit of a common cause are central to strong professional cultures (Little 1990). Teaching is a passionate vocation (Fried 1995). When Woodhead and others demean teachers' 'irrational commitments', they pluck the very heart out of teaching.

Sadly, the rhetoric and reality of educational reform in England and Wales have consistently undermined the sources of teachers' emotional as well as intellectual strength. First, as we saw earlier, educational reform has intensified teachers' work – adding huge burdens to a job that is already excessively demanding. Secondly, educational reform has also been anti-intellectual. It has failed to call upon the professional wisdom of teachers; and it has dismantled and discarded much of the expertise of educational research, regarding it as either an irksome interference or an expensive irrelevance. English and Welsh educational reform has even reshaped teacher education to make it less reflective and critical by shifting it more to the schools. But if Woodhead's words are to be believed, practice doesn't make perfect. Rather, in the title of Deborah Britzman's book, practice merely makes practice

(Britzman 1991). If strong professional cultures that embrace intellectual adventure are going to be possible among our teachers in our schools, a much less dismissive approach to the professional wisdom of teachers and to the expertise of educational research will be needed in the future.

It is not just Woodhead's words that have been flawed in their treatment of teachers and their professionalism. Ironically, indeed perversely, some researchers have argued that the inspection processes of his own agency, *Ofsted*, have actually contributed to the *deprofessionalization* of teachers. The impact of intrusive 'official' inspection on teacher stress has been noted by several authors (e.g. Brindlecombe *et al.* 1995). But the most gritty account of the 'underlife' of Ofsted inspections and their impact on teachers is to be found in qualitative research by Jeffrey and Woods (1996). The teachers who were subjected to inspection in Jeffrey and Woods's case:

> experienced fear, anguish, anger, despair, depression, humiliation, gr   nd guilt ... they showed signs of loss of confidence in the fully professional role, feelings of inadequacy, diminution of status, dehumanisation, reduced autonomy, weakened commitment.
>
> [p. 11]

The emotional politics of educational inspection among the teachers subjected to it are revealed in the following quotes from the study:

> However confident you are as a teacher, you know that you could do bett if you had more energy, if there were two of you, if you had two heads and seven arms. Because you are instrumental in the growth of these children ... you are always going to feel a failure ... [Ofsted] makes you reflect. It makes you look at yourself very hard and you say, 'Yes I'm not very good at that' or 'I didn't do enough of that' ... Whatever criticism they make, it's going to feel ... that the last 20 years have been for nothing. It's not about what progress schools have made in the last 15 years. It's 'Schools fail', 'Head to be removed', 'Hit-team going in'. It doesn't matter what you look at, it's about failure in schools ...
>
> I can't work any harder than I'm working at the moment. It's impossible. If it gets worse, I might as well get out ... I think you have to prioritise your life and this has really made me focus on the fact that I have the wrong priorities. Work, career – life's too short. My priorities have been geared up towards work. I'm not willing to give any more of myself to this profession as a human being. I think they've taken enough ... It really has made me think about who I am as a person ...
>
> We have to be valued for ourselves, otherwise there is a breakdown ... All these schemes of work have taken the control of teaching out of my hands. I have to fit into this. It's like a bereavement when people die you feel unenthusiastic! There is a bereavement for a way of teaching. It is now completely out of my control. Ofsted is a realisation of what is taking over.

In response to critiques of the intrusive inspection process, Mr Woodhead has retorted that they come from 'those who purport to speak for teachers rather than teachers themselves' (*Times Educational Supplement* 20 April 1996: 19). However, his own body's evidence (on which he pins high credibility) that 83.5 per cent of headteachers are satisfied by their experience of inspection, curiously rests on data drawn from managers and not the teachers who work for them. On a range of issues (especially those that add strength to their managerial bow), school managers (i.e. headteachers) typically take a much more positive view of imposed educational reform than their classroom teachers do (e.g. Bishop and Mulford 1996). The words of despair and rebuke we have quoted above, however, are definitely those of classroom teachers themselves – words that qualitative research can help bring to the printed page, in the public domain, in ways that administrative surveys never really can. Surveys give no voice to ordinary teachers. They only permit senior administrators like Mr Woodhead to speak presumptuously (and often less than generously) on behalf of those teachers – to put their own judgemental spin on the numerical data, that is.

If it is time to renew the purpose, passions and practices of teaching, it is time to review the role that external inspection plays in this process, so that internal review accompanies external inspection (Cuttance 1995), and so that inspection becomes part of a new process of rigorous and thoughtful conversation and dialogue, not one of incontestable judgement and hierarchical critique.

Teachers as failures

A second approach to educational change that has rapidly gained ascendancy in the post-Reform Act era is that of identifying 'failing schools' and of deploying strategies to 'turn them round' or close them down altogether if necessary. Politically and administratively, the 'failing schools' initiative was nested within the previous Government's Improving Schools programme, the work of the Department for Education's School Effectiveness division, and the regular school inspection reports of the ⬤ e for Standards in Education (Ofsted). By October 1995, around 80 schools in E   nd had been identified as 'failing', and corrective strategies had been initiated in many of them (Lankester 1995). Barber (1995) estimated that the number of failing schools that would eventually be identified by the end of Ofsted's first round of inspections would be somewhere between 250 and 500: about 1–2 per cent of all state funded schools in England and Wales. Strategies to deal with such 'failing schools' have included requiring the local education authority to provide a commentary on the action plan that the 'failing' school in question has to produce following its inspection. The local education authority has also been able to appoint additional governors, take over the school's budget, provide financial resources or external consultancy support to assist turnaround, or even close the school down if it sees fit.

Conceptually, issues concerning 'failing schools' are rooted within an increasingly respectable and established research tradition of school effectiveness and improvement. School effectiveness research has demonstrated how outcomes of achievement or behaviour can vary between schools dealing with similar kinds of pupil population. School improvement research, by contrast, has focused on the processes of change which seem to be central to the efforts of schools which are seeking to become more successful (Stoll and Fink 1996). Failing schools are schools that in a broad sense are perceived to be ineffective, in so far as pupils 'fail to progress as far as might be expected from a consideration of [their] intake' (Barber 1995: 5). Specifically, they are schools identified as such on the basis of Ofsted inspections of them. To turn such schools around, some writers feel that very different strategies may be needed from those which have proved successful in improving schools that are already good, or in ones that are only moderately problematic (Reynolds 1995).

Failing schools, it is suggested, should be treated as seriously as falling aeroplanes or dying patients. What such schools may need is not continuous improvement, professional collaboration, a jointly developed common vision or any other cliché of school improvement. Rather, it is felt, failing schools may need intensive care, elimination of error, attention to detail, or taking out of service altogether if necessary (e.g. Myers and Goldstein 1997). Writers have struggled to agree on appropriate metaphors and a common language to characterize school failure and its correction; but whether the images are ones of intensive care or of air traffic controller training, for example, the overall discourse of school failure has been one of mounting crisis and imminent catastrophe. This focus on failure, and the discourse through which such failure is described have been, we believe, deeply disturbing features of post-Reform Act approaches to educational change. There are several reasons for our concern. The first three of these concern the wider discourse of improvement from which springs the specific preoccupation with failure, while the last focuses on the treatment of failure itself.

First, notwithstanding its growing popularity, and its commendable endorsement in detail of many change strategies that recognize and capitalize on the professionalism of teachers (e.g. professional collaboration, and evolutionary rather than imposed planning), the overall language of school improvement in general, and expectations that teachers should commit to continuous improvement in particular, can seem condescending to these teachers. Being improved, like being developed, is a less than flattering fate. Professional makeovers, like personal makeovers, often imply poor taste or unappealing plainness among those who have been selected for them. Self-improvement is an admirable virtue, of course; but when everyone is urged to commit to continuous improvement as an unending professional obligation, then just like the children of parents who are never really satisfied, teachers can experience the agenda of improvement as one where their superiors and inspectors seem endlessly obsessed only with their imperfections.

Secondly, the rhetoric of continuous improvement can be used as an administrative lever to get teachers to comply with the constant demands of ceaseless change – change that is often ill-thought-out and insensitively imposed without teacher consultation or consent. A language that is often associated with enhancing teachers' professionalism can often be deployed, in this respect, to undermine it.

Thirdly, while researchers report that the teachers and schools most likely to commit to improvement projects are those who are already successful and feel confident enough to acknowledge their failures and imperfections as a result (Stoll and Fink 1996), the exhortation to commit to continuous improvement carries connotations of churlishness and carping dissatisfaction among researchers and administrators, for whom no amount of change and no degree of success ever seems to be enough. 'Could do better' on a pupil's report card is a depressing enough commentary, but at least there is always the prospect of being able to rectify later the performance that has given rise to the evaluation, either next term or next year. 'Could do better' as a founding principle of school improvement, however, converts such episodes of disappointment into unending existential states: a kind of professional purgatory where heaven must always wait.

Even when educational change is couched relatively positively in terms of school improvement, then, the discourse of improvement can still be experienced by teachers as condescending, and as casting aspersions on their present practice. Years of being insulted or ignored by the rhetoric of educational reform, and of being criticized constantly as a profession in the mass media, only heightens teachers' sensitivities to the negative implications that 'improvement' can carry (Tripp 1993). Perhaps we should be talking of professional learning instead of continuous improvement, and of organizational learning instead of school improvement. And perhaps, too, we should acknowledge that there are times to settle and consolidate as well as times to take risks and seek improvement. Improvement is an important obligation, but we should recognize that pursuing it should not be a relentless task without respite, and that there are moments when continuity and consolidation are as important as improvement and change.

If the discourse of improvement is problematic enough, its alter ego, failure, is more troubling still. The assault on school failure has been conducted with equal force and enthusiasm by the main political parties. It has been a tough discourse of inspection, intervention and associated threats of closure. It has conveyed the impression that standards are a priority, failure will not be tolerated, and something will be done about them. The discourse of school failure has been, in this respect, a 'macho' one of outrage, intervention and force – a discourse in which teachers' positive qualities and the need to engage them could find little space.

Yet we have seen that the proportion of schools likely to be designated as 'failing' is rather small. Of course, one failing school, like one dying patient, is one failure too many. But the proportionate scale of a problem that seems to encompass no more than 2 per cent of the nation's schools scarcely warrants the amount of attention being accorded it in governmental rhetoric and in school effectiveness and improvement research. How can we explain this disparity between a relatively small-scale problem and the high degree of professional and political attention accorded it?

Of course, among many of those concerned about 'failure' in pupils and in schools, there is a sincere wish to rectify great wrongs being committed against the most underprivileged sections of society. Those who are poor in life should not also experience impoverished schooling. This compounds one calumny with another, and to address 'failing schools' is to take positive action in favour of the most vulnerable members of the pupil body. But there is more to the recent policy preoccupation with 'failing schools' than this.

It may be that 'failing schools' and the severe treatment being meted out to them have been meant as a moral warning to other schools not to fall any further behind. This is like singling out class troublemakers as an example to the rest. Equally, it may be that shifting the public gaze to a small minority of failing schools has helped deflect attention from the needs of the majority of the nation's schools for more government funding and support, as well as greater generosity of spirit towards their teachers. The discourse of failure may also steer public attention away from teachers' and schools' achievements and successes which, had they been recognized and celebrated, might well have undermined the more politically profitable strategy of rooting out failure and other educational wickedness, so that it can be subjected to swift, decisive, visible and popular action.

Last, but not least, identifying failing schools in norm-referenced terms as the bottom percentile of all schools, resulted in the 'failing schools' persistently turning up in socially and economically disadvantaged areas – ones normally under the control of Labour education authorities (or school districts). If school failure were genuinely defined in more sophisticated and subtle ways – as failure in relation to the achievement levels that might be expected, given the social backgrounds of the school's children – even schools that are seemingly successful (when compared against all schools) might turn out to merely cruising in the slipstream of their well motivated high achievers (Stoll and Fink 1996). These cruising schools add little or no value to what their pupils bring into school with them. In a real sense, they are failing their pupils just as much as the officially 'failing' schools are. They are magnets for attracting existing ability, not motivators of true achievement. But to designate *these* schools as failures, many of which cater for the comfortably-off, in Conservative-controlled areas, would not have been quite so expedient or electorally attractive! Bullies always pick on easier targets!

None of this is to deny the importance of doing something about schools that are struggling, and whose pupils are struggling because of them. Confronting schools that are not performing well is not the issue here, however. The issues, rather, are why this problem should be dramatized as failure, what is it that counts as failure, who gets stigmatized as 'failing', and which schools are allowed to continue being complacent because the narrow definitions of difficulty (or 'failure') preclude them.

Overall, the post-Reform Act rhetoric of 'failing schools' has done no more to recognize and further the professionalism of the vast majority of teachers as supporters and instigators of positive change than the seven years and more of legislated changes in education which swept through the Thatcher years and beyond. Each strategy ignored the professionalism of teachers, highlighted their weaknesses instead of building on their strengths, and both diverted attention from and denied recognition to the many positive struggles for school success among teachers in schools which are not failing, and in circumstances that owe no debt to the legislated frameworks of educational reform.

Reform in comparative perspective

Educational reform need not be like this. It need not perseverate on teachers' failings. Nor need it exclude teachers from the creation and implementation of legislation. There are many ways to approach educational reform, and that of England and Wales is only one of them.

For instance, just across the Channel in France, the government has been promoting stronger intellectual preparation of teachers within universities as an antidote to the rampant utilitarianism of solely practical training. In Japan, meanwhile, the government has decided to build economic efficiency by moving away from a unified and uniform nationally-imposed curriculum towards much more wide-ranging diversity (Shimahara and Sakai 1995). And in Ontario, Canada, where one of the authors now lives and works, a self-regulating teachers' council or College of Teachers has been established. With its controlling body of 31 people, 17 of whom are elected teachers, it is currently designing a radically new framework for professional learning and leadership training in the province; assisting in accrediting programmes of initial teacher education; defining and maintaining professional standards for teaching; and drawing up as well as applying codes of conduct for its members.

Across the world, many other approaches to educational reform are sponsoring greater diversity in teaching and learning to accommodate conditions of rapid change and multiculturalism. These reforms accord greater discretion to teachers and schools to meet their pupils' needs by giving them significant flexibility over curriculum matters, and not just over the details of budget, administration and governance. They are often reforms that also take a more generous, respectful and inclusive stance towards teachers, instead of scapegoating them for the problem, heaping mountains of unwanted change upon them, and largely ignoring their own needs for professional learning, growth and support as part of the overall change effort.

From reform to renewal

None of the major political parties in Britain yet seems to have got to grips with these alternative approaches to educational reform. In its run-up to the 1997 general election, the Labour Party promised make-up summer-school literacy programmes, initiatives for pupils to participate in community service, expanded provision for pre-school learning and child care, and reduced class sizes in the early years of primary school. Acceptable policy items though they might be, none of these directly addresses the core activities of teaching and learning on which improvements in quality depend, nor do they tackle the question of how to support and promote professional learning for teachers. In exercising a moratorium on the National Curriculum, Labour may have tried to protect teachers from the further tribulations of imposed change. For teachers who need to catch their breath and consolidate, this may be an important step. Yet strategies of easement and indifference may not be enough to secure the renewal of teachers' spirit, energy, commitment and skills.

Policymakers must also create necessary conditions, support and initiatives if they wish teachers to pursue positive educational change themselves (Darling-Hammond 1995). For instance, significant energy and imagination might be released among those teachers and schools who still have a collective memory of how to undertake curriculum innovation and school-level change from the period preceding the National Curriculum, allowing them to apply for waivers permitting them to be excluded from the details of National Curriculum requirements as they now stand.

Labour's voice has perhaps echoed too readily the strident tones of Conservative educational policy and its preoccupation with celebrating parental choice and eliminating 'failing schools'. At a time when teachers and schools have endured years of scapegoating and stigmatization, and when they desperately need to feel they are a valued part of the solution, and not just an obstacle to Reform Act implementation, some signs of positive support and intervention from which teachers might benefit are urgently needed.

area in which support is surely needed is in meeting the professional learning needs of teachers *outside* their own schools, to build strong professional communities of teacher learning within schools and across them where teachers engage in professional dialogue, talk about practice, practice new initiatives and get moral support and feedback from colleagues as they engage in the uncertainties of change together. Years of Conservative educational policy have not only diminished the role of local state bureaucracies in the shape of the local education authority (LEA), but have also removed many of the systems of support for professional learning and curriculum consultancy that many LEAs now find more difficult to provide. Nor, when schools have been placed in market competition with each other for parental custom, have they usually been inclined to collaborate around professional learning needs, give away good ideas to their competitors, or let their colleagues in neighbouring institutions see them wash their own dirty linen in public. Some of the most valuable forms of professional learning teachers can get are those that involve connecting with colleagues in other schools, receiving feedback and ideas from consultants or 'critical friends' outside their own institution, and generally having access to other practices, ideas and advice that provide a point of comparison for and a source of reflection on their own accustomed ways of working in their own immediate setting (Little 1990).

Yet it is these very forms of professional learning that market competition and the destruction of LEA support have undermined. In recent years, professional learning has tended to focus on the short-term implementation of Government priorities, rather than on more generative investment in building learning, commitment and capacity among local communities of teachers in the quest for greater success (Day *et al*. 199 chers interviewed by Helsby and Knight (1997), for example, observe that since the 1988 Education Reform Act, very little professional development or in-service provision has enabled them to exchange ideas or generally interact with colleagues in other schools. Similarly, this study found that access to professional development has disproportionately excluded many ordinary classroom teachers and has been disproportionately concentrated among those in management positions. Conservative education policy has created a vacuum of professional learning at the local level: a key priority is surely now to fill it. Indeed, in *Beyond Left and Right*, Anthony Giddens (1995) has argued that it is through creating such generative politics at the local community level that the new struggles for democracy should be undertaken in the years ahead. There is an urgent need for visionary new policies that stimulate professional learning among teachers, and that connect it to positive educational change. In the wake of a Conservative Government that sacrificed the community to the market, finding ways to build professional community between schools and support them at the local level may not be a bad place to start afresh.

The Teacher Training Agency has begun to address some of the key issues here, by establishing and resourcing pilot projects in school-based teacher research, and by trying to achieve national consistency and direction, as well as local relevance and follow-through in continuous professional development (Mahony 1996). However, the principle that an appointed and anointed body, consisting mainly of people other than classroom teachers, can somehow create professional development and build a stronger sense of professionalism *for* teachers, seems to us to be deeply flawed. This is not least because a body appointed by Government to improve professional development *for* teachers will always have difficulty separating teachers' own long-term and continuing professional learning needs (and the structures and processes needed to fulfil them) from short-term in-service training priorities that are attached to the implementation of particular Government policies. Unless this potentially serious conflict of interest and direction about teachers' professional development can be resolved, it is always likely that teachers' pursuit of professional improvement will be outflanked by Government's need to exert political control.

One way around this problem of how to promote stronger, more effective forms of professional learning within the educational system is to establish a self-regulating professional body for teachers such as the long-advocated General Teaching Council. Should such a self-regulatory professional body come into being, it will be important that it does not degenerate into a bureaucratically bland organization which merely regulates issues of certification, dismissal and disciplinary conduct among the teaching force. One of the most powerful ways to restore teachers' faith in educational policy, and to make maximum use of the energy and wisdom that the teaching profession can potentially contribute to the change process, is to give such an organization real teeth in creating and monitoring national frameworks of professional learning for teachers and headteachers that are defined by the profession itself and not imposed by government priorities. This is not to say that Government priorities should be ignored. But they should not squeeze out commitment to effective long-term processes of continuous professional learning. Indeed, their implementation should be integrated with these long-term commitments, rather than occluding or cross-cutting them. Moreover, such implementation would be more effective if it were negotiated and channelled through the professional body, and would thereby ensure harmonization of short-term reform, existing professional cultures and long-term professional learning efforts.

Throughout all these initiatives, as well as others that might promote more and better professional learning among teachers, a new political and public discourse about teachers and teaching is needed that is more trusting and respectful of teachers and their talents. The announcement in the autumn of 1996 of a National Curriculum for teacher training in England and Wales characteristically dwelt on the shortcomings and weaknesses of teaching which the new National Curriculum would remedy. In English and Welsh educationa reform rhetoric, teachers have consistently been found wanting. But in another context, a Royal Commission on Learning in Ontario, Canada, sought to establish a different public mood about teachers and teaching by making the following declaration:

> Teachers are our heroes. We believe they should be everyone's heroes. Anyone who has watched a teacher begin a day facing a group of kids who'd rather be anywhere in the world than sitting in that classroom learning about something called geometry that they couldn't care less about, understands only too well what a frustrating, thankless, enervating task these mortal women and men face so much of their working lives. In return, they feel unappreciated, disrespected, the focus of twisted media attacks, caught in an almost war-like situation not of their making.
>
> [Ontario Royal Commission on Learning 1994: 13]

It is time to rethink our approach to educational reform. It is time for reformers to reconnect with the profession of teaching and with the expertise of educational research, by working with teachers to build strong professional cultures of shared learning, joint work and collaborative commitment. It is time for teachers to be the included vanguard of reform, and not be made its marginalized victims. It is time for a change of direction and time for a change of heart.

The organization of the book

It is in relation to this broad agenda of the need to bring teachers back into educational reform, and to put their voices and their needs for professional learning at the heart of the change process, that this book has been compiled.

The book is a product of the research being conducted within an international network of leading researchers in eight countries called Professional Actions and Cultures of Teaching (PACT), directed by Andy Hargreaves and Ivor Goodson. Our participating researchers come from Australia, Canada, England, Israel, Japan, Norway, Sweden and the USA. Our concern has been to determine what teachers' professional knowledge is, who defines it, how it can be shared, and how it can be made public. The concern is to understand what strong professional cultures look like, how they can be created and sustained, and what contribution they can make to educational reform. The chapters in this volume have been produced by several members of this PACT network, and have arisen from that network's continuous commitment to dialogue and debate.

In Chapter 2, Gary McCulloch takes the position that whilst education may hold a unique power to engineer our future in a changing world, conventional images of the past, as well as idealized images of the future, are influential in shaping the reforms being urged upon the education system. He argues that recent education policy formulation in England and Wales is based upon a highly idealized vision of the future in which past policy failures are rendered unimportant – the triumph of hope over experience. McCulloch provides a powerful critique of alternative visions of how educational policy can help create a genuine democracy. He argues that whilst these visions are politically and ideologically very different, they share significant assumptions about the way in which educational reform is seen as a means of preparing for the twenty-first century.

The idea that public education stands in a functional relationship to society as it is, has to be set alongside the view that it can engineer and shape the nature and quality of future social relations. These two notions, he argues, remain as resilient as ever as key rationales for continued public investment in education.

In McCulloch's view, alternative critiques of education policy have tended to render the past negatively, in order to justify a basis of rethinking education policy. The past, he suggests, has been posited as the problem to which the solution is the future. Such a view rejects the opportunity to learn something of the processes of change and reform in social life – as well as continuity and tradition – through grounded, historical experience. McCulloch argues that we will be able to explore the social engineering and functional notions of educational change better if we take proper ownership of our historical experience. In this regard, efforts to create schools and teachers for the next century can make constructive use of experience we have gained since the last one.

In Chapter 3, Ivor Goodson explores the relationship between theoretical knowledge, educational research and teacher professionalism. By focusing on the recent history of educational policymaking within which theoretical knowledge and educational research have been marginalized, he argues that the fate of the theorist is reflected in the fate of the classroom teacher. There are echoes of McCulloch's chapter in so far as educational research of the past is commonly seen as part of the problem rather than as part of the solution to creating effective teachers in effective schools. Goodson argues that if we reject theoretical bodies of knowledge and reflective actions based upon research studies, we will fail to move beyond an uncritical and unreflective implementation of practices defined by others. This cuts at the roots of teacher motivation which Day, in his chapter, sees as highly significant in creating professionals for the twenty-first century. To ignore theory and research is to ignore some of the basic forms of expertise on which policy should be founded. These, Goodson argues, are central to the development of teacher professionalism and are crucial in confirming the public's perception that teaching is a professional activity. They form part of the means of maintaining or reviving a collaborative and theoretical mission through which new strength and vigour can be brought to teachers' actions.

In the chapter by Chris Day, the challenge for teaching in the twenty-first century is set within the context of a renewed vision of society, schooling and teaching. His basic argument is that teachers and teaching are central to the creation of a world within which the capacities of future citizens to adapt to change, embrace it and actively contribute to it, will be significant dispositions at the start of the new millennium. The social task, he says, is to attract the best minds and spirits into teaching, and to restore a sense of worth to the promotion of lifelong learning opportunities for all. Any real sense of future, Day argues, can be too easily sacrificed on the altar of short-term policy formulation, within which teachers are denied the opportunity to own their own professionalism   with children, so with teachers: the key to developing a successful learning culture is motivation. Teachers, it is argued, need to be freed of the derision and criticism which has been so much a part of the public discourse on schools for more than a decade. If schools of the future are to become secure places within which the necessary future dispositions of pupils can be developed, society will require teachers who are not only competent but also idealistic, confident of their personal worth, and who are supported through careerlong development opportunities. Such teachers are central to the vision of reconstructed education which can deliver to the vision of social 'good'. To such ends, Day emphasizes the role that idealism must play within the overarching moral commitment of teachers to pupils and schools. The main agenda for continuing professional development, he concludes, should be concerned with creating and sustaining such moral and professional purposes.

In his chapter on self-managing and self-governing schools, Brian Caldwell offers a strategic analysis of what is necessary to professionalize the cultures of teaching further. The analysis is presented in a form of nine contentions, with a concluding synthesis suggesting what the future may hold. On the basis of international research, Caldwell argues that self-management is probably long overdue and is likely to be an irreversible trend. Whilst heads of schools have largely accepted Local Management of Schools – characterized as it is by greater transparency in the resources schools receive and why – these reforms, he argues, have failed to impact on the ordinary class teacher. A key contention in his chapter is not simply that self-management should be accepted, but that its operationalization requires reforms of organizational structures as well as redefining teaching as something more flexible than a 'job'.

Milbrey McLaughlin's chapter on rebuilding teacher professionalism in the USA reveals fascinating parallels with, but also crucial differences from, the reform agenda in England and Wales. The American experience underlines the fact that concern over teacher professionalism and teacher action transcends national boundaries, and is driven by a shared desire to improve the quality of student learning and standards of schooling.

McLaughlin shows how the perceived mismatch in the USA between what society expects and what students can do has unleashed a flood of initiatives aimed at raising standards, changing curriculum, hardening accountability and restructuring the way in which schools function. Much of this will be recognizable within the English and Welsh context in the wake of the 1988 Education Reform Act. In the USA as in Britain, efforts at standard-setting have generated the need for teachers to own new conceptions of how they teach and how they assess pupil learning. Teachers now have to learn to teach in ways in which they have not been taught themselves.

These reforms have set an agenda for professional learning which carries with it a new concept of pre- and post-experience training. The new paradigm recognizes the importance of embedding teachers' learning in everyday activities. With children and teachers, successful professional development is seen to emerge from continuous reflection on practice and through collaboration with other practitioners. Critical to rebuilding teacher professionalism, McLaughlin argues, are opportunities and organizational arrangements which enable teachers to rethink the technical culture of how teaching is best done, and to re-examine their expectations for pupils as well as their own roles.

Ken Shimahara explores the intriguing issue of what lessons Japanese educational reform might hold for educational reform in England and Wales. Japanese education, he shows, while often subject to stereotypes of overheated competition and achievement, also rests squarely on strong social and moral bonds that Japanese teachers establish with their pupils. The affective as well as the cognitive sides of educational change and reform are extremely important in the Japanese context. More than this, while Japanese education is often held up as an exemplary model for Western educational systems to emulate, it is clear that the problem addressed by educational reformers in Japan is actually one of excessive uniformity in its systems of curriculum and testing which meshes poorly with the demands of a post-modern, post-industrial society for greater diversity and technological innovation. It is paradoxical, Shimahara observes, that English and Welsh educational reform has been trying to minimize diversity in the cause of securing greater standardization, when Japan is seeking to achieve exactly the opposite.

In the final chapter, Andy Hargreaves moves beyond the problems of coping with imposed educational reform in England and Wales, to address the challenge of achieving continuous, school-generated change, in a social context that is often paradoxical and unreasonable in the demands and expectations it places upon teachers. Hargreaves explores what it means for teachers to work within a world of paradox, and outlines six dimensions of school change in the post-modern age that need to be addressed simultaneously as teachers work individually and collectively to bring about positive change and achieve professional and educational renewal in such difficult times. These dimensions are the purpose of teaching, the passions of teaching, policy realization, school culture, school structure and organizational learning.

We hope that these chapters, focused on educational reform in Britain but drawn from across the world in order to address it, will together stimulate dialogue and reflection among teachers, administrators and policymakers about how to bring about positive educational change in our complex, diverse, rapidly changing post-modern times. We also hope that they will help create a space for teachers' voices to come together and be heard again in the ongoing struggle for positive educational change that achieves high standards of teaching, learning and caring for all.

References

Acker, S. (1995) Gender and teachers' work, in M. Apple (ed.) *Review of Research in Education*, 21. Washington, D.C.: AERA.

Ball, S. and Bowe, R. (1992) Subject departments and the implementation of the national curriculum. *Journal of Curriculum Studies*, 24: 97–116.

Barber, M. (1995) The dark side of the moon: Imagining an end to failure in urban education. The TES/Greenwich Education Lecture, *Times Educational Supplement*.

Best, R. (1994) Teachers' supportive roles in a secondary school: A case study and discussion. *Support for Learning*, 9(4), November.

Bishop, R. and Mulford, W. (1996) Empowerment in four primary schools: They don't really care. *International Journal of Educational Reform*, 5(2): 193–204.

Brindlecombe, N., Ormston, M. and Shaw, M. (1995) Teachers' perceptions of school inspection; a stressful experience. *Cambridge Journal of Education*, 25(1).

Britzman, D. (1991) *Practice Makes Practice*. Albany: SUNY Press.

Campbell, R.J. and Neill, S.R. (1994) *Primary Teachers at Work*. London: Routledge.

Cooper, C. (1994) *The Guardian*, 18 November.

Cuttance, P. (1995) An evaluation of quality management. *Cambridge Journal of Education*, 25(1).

Darling-Hammond, L. (1995) Policy for restructuring, in A. Lieberman (ed.) *The Work of Restructuring Schools*. New York: Teachers College Press.

Day, C., Hall, C., Gammage, P. and Coles, M. (1993) *Leadership and Curriculum in the Primary School*. London: Paul Chapman Publishing.

Elliott, J. (1991) *Action Research for Educational Change*. Milton Keynes: Open University Press.

Fried, R. (1995) *The Passionate Teacher*. Boston: Beacon Press.

Fullan, M. and Hargreaves, A. (1996) *What's Worth Fighting for in Your School*, 2nd edn. New York: Teachers College Press; Buckingham: Open University Press.

Giddens, A. (1995) *Beyond Left and Right*. Cambridge: Polity Press.

Hargreaves, A. (1994) *Changing Teachers, Changing Times: Teachers' Work and Culture in the Postmodern Age*. London: Cassell; New York: Teachers College Press; Toronto: OISE Press.

Hargreaves, A. (1997) Rethinking educational change, in A. Hargreaves (ed.) *Rethinking Educational Change with Heart and Mind, The 1997 ASCD Yearbook*. Alexandria, Va: The Association for Supervision and Curriculum Development.

Hargreaves, D. (1995) Inspection and school improvement. *Cambridge Journal of Education*, 25(1).

Helsby, G. and Knight, P. (1997) Continuing professional development and the National Curriculum, in G. McCulloch and G. Helsby (eds) *Teachers and the National Curriculum*. London: Cassell.

Helsby, G. and McCulloch, G. (1996) Teacher professionalism and curriculum control, in I. Goodson and A. Hargreaves (eds) *Teachers' Professional Lives*. New York: Falmer Press.

Jeffrey, R. and Woods, P. (1996) Feeling deprofessionalized: The social construction of emotions during an OFSTED inspection, *Cambridge Journal of Education*.

Lankester, T. (1995) National challenge that we can all be proud of, *Times Educational Supplement*, 6 October.

Little, J.W. (1990) The persistence of privacy: Autonomy and initiative in teachers' profes-
    sional relations. *Teachers' College Record*, 91(4): 509–36.

Mahony, P. (1996) Trailing the TTA, paper presented at British Educational Research
    Association Conference, University of Lancaster, 13–17 September.

Myers, K. and Goldstein, H. (1997) Failing schools in a failing system?, in A. Hargreaves
    (ed.) *Positive Change for School Success, The 1997 ASCD Yearbook*. Alexandria, Va:
    The Association for Supervision and Curriculum Development.

Nias, J. (1989) *Primary Teachers Talking*. London: Routledge and Kegan Paul.

Ontario Royal Commission on Learning (1994) *For the Love of Learning*, short version.
    Toronto: Queen's Printer.

Reynolds, D. (1995) 'The problem of the ineffective school: Some evidence and some
    speculations', unpublished paper. Economic and Social Research Council Seminar.

Rosenholtz, S. (1989) *Teachers' Workplace*. New York: Longman.

Shimahara, K. and Sakai, A. (1995) *Learning to Teach in Two Cultures*. New York: Garland
    Publishing.

Stoll, L. and Fink, D. (1996) *Changing Our Schools*. Buckingham: Open University Press.

Talbert, J.E. and McLaughlin, M. (1994) Teacher professionalism in local school contexts.
    American Journal of Education, 102 (February): 123–53.

Tripp, D. (1993) *Critical Incidents in Teaching: Developing Professional Judgement*. New
    York: Routledge.

Webb, J. and Vulliamy, G. (1996) A deluge of directives. *British Educational Research
    Journal*, 22(4).

Woodhead, C. (1995) Education – the illusive engagement and the continuing frustration,
    Times Educational Supplement. 1st Annual Lecture to HM Chief Inspectors.

Woods, P. (1993) *Critical Events in Teaching and Learning*. London: Falmer Press.

2 MARKETING THE MILLENNIUM: EDUCATION FOR THE TWENTY-FIRST CENTURY

Gary McCulloch

Educational reforms are built partly upon our images of the future, the kinds of future that we would wish for or detest. In the rethinking of education in England and Wales, images of the future, and more specifically of the twenty-first century, are currently having a particularly marked effect upon the kinds of reform that are being put forward. Education holds a unique power, in our imaginations, to engineer our future in the changed world of the new millennium. On the other hand, the past tends to be overshadowed by the promise of the future. This chapter reviews some of the chief characteristics of the new millenarianism as it has affected educational reform in England and Wales in the 1990s, focusing on its limitations and dangers as well as on the inherent promise that it offers.

A powerful and cogent metaphor for change is involved in the idea of turning over a new leaf to meet the fresh needs of the twenty-first century, and it is attractive to believe in the notion of developing a rational and comprehensive blueprint that will serve this purpose (e.g. Hicks and Holden 1995; Dalin and Rust 1996). The transformative impact of the new technologies and the image of the dawn of a new 'post-modernist' epoch (e.g. Hargreaves 1994) tend strongly to underline these possibilities for the future in a way that can make them appear to be almost limitless. Such images can be used constructively in order to develop coherent and inspiring visions for radical, holistic reform. At the same time, however, they often suffer from two characteristic problems. First, they are prone to idealize the future, to build castles in the air that contrast starkly with the intractable dilemmas of the imperfect present. They involve a quasi-utopian discourse that generates high expectations for radical and fundamental change. It seems likely that this tendency may lead in turn to disappointment and alienation if there is a failure to deliver or to benefit from reform. Secondly, they tend to overlook or ignore the continuities inherited from the past, or else to 'telescope' the past in order to draw simple and finished conclusions to particular problems that need to be resolved. In both respects they serve as a marketing device to promote the new possibilities of education in a new century, designed to appeal to consumers of different kinds who are grown weary of the old familiar product.

The characteristic tendency to idealize education in the twenty-first century is reflected, for example, in the report of the National Commission on Education, *Learning to Succeed*, especially in its notion of 'twenty-first century teachers':

> In our vision, a teacher in the twenty-first century will be an authority and enthusiast in the knowledge, ideas, skills, understanding and values to be presented to pupils. The teacher will be an expert on effective learning, with knowledge of a range of classroom methods that can be intelligently applied and understanding of appropriate organisational and management styles, conditions and resources.

It continues in the same vein:

> The teacher will have the capacity to think deeply about educational aims and values, and thereby critically about educational programmes. The teacher will be willing to motivate and encourage each and every pupil, assessing progress and learning needs in their widest sense, even when this involves them in areas outside formal education.

And it concludes:

> The teacher will in the first instance be an educator, not only of the 'subject' being taught but also aiming to extend the intellectual, imaginative, inquiring and critical powers of his or her pupils, and to encourage them to question their wider personal and social values.
>
> [National Commission on Education 1993: 196–7.]

These are all worthy and laudable aims, and are helpful in the way that they indicate a particular direction for the role of teachers, but the general image evoked is a highly idealized version of education in the twenty-first century (see also e.g. Barber 1996, esp. ch.8).

The changing needs of the future are also commonly invoked as a reason for insisting upon radical reforms of the education system. These novel challenges, including the need to compete in the global economy of the twenty-first century, comprise the stick to be put alongside the carrot as an incentive for change. In his highly revealing memoirs *The Turbulent Years*, the former Secretary of State for Education who was chiefly responsible for the ████ation Reform Act of 1988, Kenneth Baker, notes that: 'For a variety of reasons the education system needed radical change if it was to match the needs of twenty-first-century Britain. If this meant forgoing the usual snail's pace on which reform in education was conducted, then so be it' (Baker 1993: 169). This also helped to justify the introduction of city technology colleges, since, he argued, 'We had to educate the young of today for the jobs of tomorrow. The curriculum would therefore need to be technologically-orientated and involve employers and industralists' (Baker 1993: 171).

A further aspect of the image of the future in the reforms of the 1980s and 1990s was that it provided a means of presenting the new reforms as ushering in a new era of success and prosperity. The White Paper *Education and Training for the 21st Century* provided few details of the long-term future, but gave a firm promise that 'Our plans will meet the needs of the next decade and the next century.' For young people, they would 'offer the means of qualifying for careers with good prospects and job satisfaction' – while also creating 'better opportunities for young people from all backgrounds, of both sexes, from inner cities and elsewhere'. In the case of employers, they would offer 'the means of working with education and training providers to produce skilled and motivated young people who will make a real contribution to the success of their companies and local communities'. For the '21st century economy', meanwhile, 'they offer the prospect of a workforce with first class skills to produce the wealth on which our society depends for its standard of living' (DES, DoE, Welsh Office 1991: 64). The twenty-first century, it seemed, would offer something for everybody, on condition that current policies were supported and maintained intact.

Laying claim to the future in this way therefore meant casting it in the image of the present. The White Paper *Choice and Diversity*, published in 1992, suggested that the new reforms being introduced would provide 'a new and evolutionary framework for the organisation of our schools, robust enough to last well into the next century' (D for E, Welsh Office 1992: 2). In particular, since as it asserted, 'The demands of the new century will require schools which can adapt to the changing needs of their pupils, communities and the economy', this would mean the encouragement of 'a wider diversity of schools' (D for E, Welsh Office 1992: 43). In the case of Wales, it is worth noting, the reform promised a subtly different future, as 'the basis of a prosperous, successful and *culturally rich* environment in the 21st century' (emphasis added; D for E, Welsh Office 1992: 58). In general, however, as the White Paper emphasized in its final chapter, the outcome would be 'a new century of excellence'. It claimed that

> By the next century, we will have achieved a system characterised not by uniformity but by choice, underpinned by the spread of grant-maintained schools. There will be a rich array of schools and colleges, all teaching the National Curriculum and playing to their strengths, allowing parents to choose the schools best fitted to their children's needs, and all enjoying parity of esteem.

Indeed, it added, 'The education system of the 21st century will be neither divisive nor based on some lowest common denominator. Diversity, choice and excellence will be its hallmarks, with each child having an opportunity to realise his or her full potential, liberating and developing his or her talents' (D for E, Welsh Office 1992: 64). This vision of the future, therefore, projected the dominant priorities of the 1990s into the future to propose a logical culmination of progress in the education of the twenty-first century.

These notions of the future present the twenty-first century as a blank canvas, upon which may be projected the hopes and fears of the present. They also serve to facilitate a disregarding of the past, since it appears that the problems that afflicted education in the nineteenth and twentieth centuries will somehow cease to exist after the year 2000. The corollary of this is that cultural, social and political issues tend to be dismissed as 'historical' in nature, or simply as 'out of date'. Compromise and failure are consigned to the ▓▓▓▓ An interesting example of this approach is the rehabilitation of the idea of 'p▓▓ty of esteem' between the academic and vocational. This is a notion, encouraged especially in the Spens Report of 1938, which was tested to destruction in the 1940s and 1950s. It is again an important and respectable aspiration, however, in the reforms of the 1980s and 1990s. The historical failure of 'parity of esteem' is rendered unimportant and irrelevant through a focus upon an idealized future. Thus, in *Education and Training for the 21st Century*, there should be 'equal status for academic and vocational education'. This meant that 'Young people should be free at 16 to choose the education or training options which suit them best. They should not be limited by out-of-date distinctions between qualifications or institutions' (DES, DoE, Welsh Office 1991: 24). Or again: 'Choice between the academic and vocational routes is confused by the institutional divide between further education colleges and sixth forms. Some of these differences are historical. We intend to remove those which are no longer justified' (DES, DoE, Welsh Office 1991: 25). The White Paper therefore exuded confidence that new policies would 'remove the remaining barriers to equal status between the so-called academic and vocational routes' (DES, DoE, Welsh Office 1991). The then Prime Minister, John Major, also added his seal of approval to this view: 'With the introduction of a new Advanced Diploma, we will end the artificial divide between academic and vocational qualifications, so that young people can pursue the kind of education that best suits their needs' (DES, DoE, Welsh Office 1991: Foreword). In a literal sense, this represents the triumph of hope over experience, a preference for trusting in the virgin future, rather than dwelling on the sullied past.

The spectacular comeback of the idea of parity of esteem between different types of secondary school, reflected in the White Paper *Choice and Diversity*, also highlights this tendency. Even though it distanced itself from the connotations of the 1940s, and tried to emphasize the potential significance of the National Curriculum, *Choice and Diversity* revived the same language of parity of esteem. This was no less evident in the final Dearing Report on the National Curriculum and its assessment, published at the beginning of ▓▓▓. The Dearing Report recommended that the National Curriculum should be 'slimmed down', and that 'alternative pathways' should be developed from the age of 14. These pathways would be academic, vocational, and occupational respectively, and they should be 'of equal quality, leading to parity of esteem' (Dearing 1994: para 3.19). There is an especially resonant echo here of the hopes that were voiced, and were soon frustrated, in the 1940s and 1950s (McCulloch 1994a). The later Report, also by Sir Ron Dearing, on qualifications for 16- to 19-year-olds, again maintains an emphasis on developing parity of esteem between different kinds of knowledge and skills to meet the challenges of the next century (Gleeson and Hodkinson 1995; Dearing 1996).

The renewed appeal of 'parity of esteem' in the 1990s may be partly explained in relation to its use as an administrative device, as a convenient method of divorcing education policy from wider social and historical problems. In this sense, it contributes to a 'technical fix' of deep-seated dilemmas, attempting to draw a line as it were beneath the failures of past generations. This approach is essentially ahistorical, for it ignores as irrelevant the failures of similar attempts at reform in the past, and yet tripartite divisions between 'grammar', 'technical', and 'modern' curricula and institutions have been highly resilient in changing circumstances throughout the past century (McCulloch 1995b). It is by no means self-evident that these distinctions, and the inequalities that they have reflected and encouraged, will cease to be a potent influence on educational provision in the twenty-first century.

Some critical commentaries of current educational reforms sketch alternative visions of the twenty-first century that are said to depend on developing a different kind of education policy. Sally Tomlinson, for example, argues that current reforms, which represent 'the most comprehensive reworking of the education system since the 1940s', are based on 'an ideology more appropriate to the nineteenth than the twenty-first century' (Tomlinson 1994: 1, 3). She observes that the reforms of the 1980s and 1990s have been strongly influenced by a nineteenth-century liberal individualism supplemented by a nineteenth-century moral authoritarianism and nostalgic imperialism, and concludes: 'This ideology, and its developing educational framework and content, is narrow, backward-looking, and potentially disastrous in both economic and social terms for young British people about to move into the twenty-first century' (Tomlinson 1994: 4). Against this, Tomlinson asserts an 'alternative model' that will embrace the future, as being 'appropriate to the twenty-first century, not nostalgic yearning for the nineteenth'. Children starting school in the 1990s, on this view, 'deserve a new vision', apparently because they 'will live to the year 2070 and beyond'. This 'new vision' would be built on a notion of 'genuine democracy' in which individuals must come together as a society: 'The system of education will express and create the values and framework of an educated democracy' (Tomlinson 1994: 4–5).

Tomlinson's vision of education in the twenty-first century is similar to that developed in a self-styled 'Alternative White Paper' entitled *Education: A Different Vision*, produced by the Institute for Public Policy Research (IPPR). This work strongly criticizes the then Government's White Paper, *Choice and Diversity*, and seeks to provide a more detailed notion of the likely demands of the twenty-first century. 'High quality education', it claims, 'can help shape the future' (Institute for Public Policy Research 1993: 7). The next century would demand a blend of 'distinctive individualism' and 'the capacity for harmonious co-operation'. Preparation for the twenty-first century would also involve 'the acquisition of knowledge, skills, attitudes and appropriate patterns of behaviour' that would mean the development of life-long education and more effective processes of teaching and learning (Institute for Public Policy Research 1993: 8–12).

These ideas of education for the twenty-first century are clearly very different, politically and ideologically, from those of the then Government. In some respects, even so, there are important similarities between them. Both use the twenty-first century as a means of promoting their own favoured ideals and trends and projecting these forward into the future. Both use the imminent arrival of the new millennium as a rhetorical device to emphasize the urgency of educational reform in the present; they remind us not only that the year 2000 is almost upon us, but also that those who are now entering the education system will not complete their formal education until the early years of the next century. As the matter is expressed in the White Paper *Choice and Diversity*, 'a child tested at the age of 7 this year [1992] will not be taking GCSE until 2001' (D for E, Welsh Office 1992: 64). Similarly, the IPPR reminds us that 'Children who are in school today will only be in their teens or early twenties when the 21st century dawns' (Institute for Public Policy Research 1993: 7). The same message has also been invoked with regard to university students by Anne Wright, vice-chancellor at the University of Sunderland: 'The first graduates of the new century will soon be moving on to GCSE programmes, and the first new entrants to twenty-first century higher education are now embarking on their first year of secondary schooling' (Wright 1994: 87). This invocation of the need of pupils and students who are already in the education system to be prepared for the new world of the twenty-first century increases the moral force of arguments in favour of fundamental educational reforms.

These projections of education in the twenty-first century also share some highly significant assumptions about the sense in which educational reform is a means of preparing for the new century. They convey the idea of education as a preparation for a changing society; if society is changing, education must follow suit. In other words, a functional relationship is assumed in which education serves the needs of society. At the same time, they suggest that by developing education in a particular way, the nature of the wider society will be systematically reformed in a linear and straightforward fashion. That is, the assumption is made that education is an efficient means of social engineering. It can 'help shape the future', and indeed help to engineer the shape of all of our futures. These two notions – on the one hand, that education stands in a functional relationship to society, and on the other, that education can shape the future of society – have been perhaps the two key rationales for the public project of education in the nineteenth and twentieth centuries. It appears that they remain as resilient as ever, being virtually taken for granted as we approach the new millennium.

The visions of the past that were suggested in these contemporary notions of reform also have much in common. In the 1980s, the past came to be viewed negatively rather than in terms of providing solid foundations for further development. The past was the problem, to which the solution was the future. An image of the past as barren wilderness, filled with disappointments, betrayals and failures, led directly to the major cycle of educational reform policies of the late 1980s, which attempted to change the culture of schooling itself. At the same time, there developed an ahistorical notion of educational reform, what might be described as the 'technical fix'. On this view, education policy was a technical, managerial issue, focused narrowly on the redressing of particular, narrowly defined problems, and therefore seen as unrelated to wider social, cultural and historical concerns (e.g. McCulloch 1994b).

The hostile, negative view of educational history tended to mean that it was simplified and telescoped, used mainly to explain problems and failures. In particular, the 'educational establishment' responsible for the development of the system was viewed as untrustworthy, as being itself part of the problem that needed solving. The Norwood Report of 1943 became a symbol of the general emphasis upon academic and liberal values in English education, which several historians associated with the relative decline of British industry and economic productivity (e.g. Wiener 1981; Barnett 1986; Aldcroft 1992). The Plowden Report of 1967 similarly became a symbol of the alleged excesses of 'progressive' education (see McCulloch 1994a). Sometimes, too, there was apparent a selective policy amnesia that all too often degenerated into something more serious, as policies rose without trace to supplant those which had taken priority only a few months before. These trends reflected a decline in confidence in a progressive public past in education, together with an increasing politicization in its use (see McCulloch 1997). The recourse to images of the twenty-first century can perhaps be viewed as providing an alternative to this public past in the form of a more comforting mirror for the present, allowing a notion of progress towards a better future while avoiding too close a view of the frustrations and failures that have marked the historical record of education in the twentieth century.

In these circumstances, there seems a particular need to insist upon a more substantial sense of history that may help to inform our understanding of education, and of the prospects for reform, in the years ahead. This should seek to develop frameworks for understanding that will be contestable and open to debate, but should not be seen as in any way marginal to the issues of the present and the future. In some ways, such 'lessons of the past' may be conceived as having a negative rationale. As Gosden has noted in this country, and Tyack in the United States, an awareness of history can help educational policymakers to avoid 're-inventing the wheel' (e.g. Gosden 1984; Tyack 1991, 1995; Judd 1993). It can also help to challenge current orthodoxies, as Mathieson and Bernbaum have aptly suggested, by placing them 'in a context which treats the current prescriptions and recommendations as themselves problematic, and as being at risk precisely because the level of analysis from which they begin is inadequate'. It might thus enable 'a somewhat different view to be taken of recent concerns and recommendations and hence of their likelihood of success where so many others have previously failed' (Mathieson and Bernbaum 1988: 127).

At the same time, some more positive aspects to a strongly historical dimension might also be noted. For instance, it should help in restoring a sense of education in its wider cultural, social and philosophical relationships, as was noticed much more in the reforms of the 1940s, and thus to question the technical–rational–administrative model of education policy that has been particularly influential over the past decade.

It should also provide an invaluable resource for policy and planning to be able to take advantage of the experience gained of the problems and possibilities of public education over the past two centuries. We should be able to ask ourselves: what have we learned from this very long-term project as it has developed over that time? We might approach this question in terms of an evaluation of policy and its implementation. It might be described as a kind of grounded theory – grounded, that is, in historical experience, including that of people who have been actively involved in teaching and learning throughout their own lifetimes.

Two issues in particular might be examined as part of the rediscovery of our historical experience. The first is the notion of education as a means of social engineering. This has been an underlying assumption that has helped to motivate the project of public education since the early years of the nineteenth century, and as has been seen, it continues to underpin ideas about education for the twenty-first century. To what extent does our historical experience support this notion? Does it suggest a direct, linear, straightforward relationship between the aims and social outcomes of schooling and other forms of public education? Or does it suggest a more complex interaction between education and society, which takes account of tensions between policy and practice, and of competition between a number of groups and ideologies? Similarly, the notion of education being in a functional relationship to society needs also to be explored by making greater use of our historical experience. Thus, for example, the assumption that technical education serves the needs of employers and the economy can be empirically tested, as it were, through examination of the many different initiatives in this area over the past century and more (e.g. McCulloch 1995a). Investigation of such issues for the purposes of policy and planning may help us to understand the inherent limitations of education, as well as to comprehend the hopes that made schooling and other educational institutions possible in the first place and which have sustained them for so long. It might also provide a gauge by which to register and interpret the high hopes that have characteristically been associated with educational expansion and the investment that is involved in this, and perhaps also to forestall the disappointments that have also become so regular a feature.

Rethinking education, then, should not mean building castles in the air, nor yet casting the future in our own image. Nor should the creation of schools and teachers for the twenty-first century resemble a marketing exercise in which the infinite possibilities of the millennium are packaged in alternative ways for consumers of the future. It should involve constructive and articulate use of the experience gained in the nineteenth and twentieth centuries that will enable the hopes and challenges of the twenty-first century to be measured and anticipated, as far as possible, through the experience gained from the public education project of the past 200 years.

References

Aldcroft, D. (1992) *Education, Training and Economic Performance 1944 to 1990*. Manchester: Manchester University Press.

Baker, K. (1993) *The Turbulent Years: My Life in Politics*. London: Faber and Faber.

Barber, M. (1996) *The Learning Game: Arguments for a Learning Revolution*. London: Gollancz.

Barnett, C. (1986) *The Audit of War*. London: Macmillan.

Dalin, P. and Rust, V. (eds) (1996) *Towards Education for the Twenty-First Century*. London: Cassell.

Dearing, R. (1994) *Final Report: The National Curriculum and Its Assessment*. London: SCAA.

Dearing, R. (1996) *Review of Qualifications for 16- to 19-Year-Olds*. London: SCAA.

Department for Education, Welsh Office (1992) *Choice and Diversity: A New Framework for Schools*, Cm. 2021. London: HMSO.

Department of Education and Science, Department of Employment, Welsh Office (1991) *Education and Training for the Twenty-First Century*, vol. 1, Cm. 1536. London: HMSO.

Gleeson, D. and Hodkinson, P. (1995) Ideology and curriculum policy: GNVQ and mass post-compulsory education in England and Wales. *British Journal of Education and Work*, 8(3): 5–19.

Gosden, P. (1984) National policy and the rehabilitation of the practical: the context, in D. Layton (ed.) *The Alternative Road: The Rehabilitation of the Practical*. Leeds: University of Leeds.

Hargreaves, A. (1994) *Changing Teachers, Changing Times: Teachers' Work and Culture in the Post-Modern Age*. London: Cassell.

Hicks, D. and Holden, C. (1995) *Visions of the Future: Why We Need to Teach for the Future*. Stoke-on-Trent: Trentham.

Institute for Public Policy Research (1993) *Education: A Different Vision. An Alternative White Paper*. London: IPPR.

Judd, J. (1993) Wishful thinking, Mr Major. *Independent*, 21 October.

Mathieson, M. and Bernbaum, G. (1988) The British disease: A British tradition? *British Journal of Educational Studies*, 26(2): 126–74.

McCulloch, G. (1994a) *Educational Reconstruction: The 1944 Education Act and the 21st Century*. London: Woburn Press.

McCulloch, G. (1994b) *Technical Fix? City Technology Colleges*, Education for Capability Research Group Occasional Publication no. 7. Leeds: University of Leeds.

McCulloch, G. (1995a) From education to work: The case of technical schools. *World Yearbook of Education 1995: Youth, Education and Work*. London: Kogan Page.

McCulloch, G. (1995b) The power of three: 'parity of esteem' and the social history of tripartism, in E.W. Jenkins (ed.) *Studies in the History of Education*. Leeds: Leeds University Press.

McCulloch, G. (1997) Privatising the past? History and education policy in the 1990s. *British Journal of Educational Studies*, 45(1): 69–82.

National Commission on Education (1993) *Learning to Succeed*. London: Heinemann.

Tomlinson, S. (1994) Introduction: Educational reforms – ideologies and visions, in S. Tomlinson (ed.) *Educational Reform and Its Consequences*. London: Institute for Public Policy Research/Rivers Oram Press.

Tyack, D. (1991) Public school reform: Policy talk and institutional practice. *American Journal of Education*, 100(1): 1–19.

Tyack, D. and Cuban, L. (1995) *Tinkering Toward Utopia: A Century of Public School Reform*. Cambridge, Mass.: Harvard University Press.

Wiener, M. (1981) *English Culture and the Decline of the Industrial Spirit, 1850–1980*. Cambridge: CUP.

Wright, A. (1994) The university in the community, in National Commission on Education/ Council for Industry and Higher Education *Universities in the Twenty-First Century*. London: NCE.

3 'TRENDY THEORY' AND TEACHER PROFESSIONALISM

Ivor Goodson

Will Hutton recently argued that 'the parlous condition of the country is no accident, it is the consequence of a misguided project informed by a misguided theory' (Hutton 1994). With regard to education, I would argue that the parlous condition of public schooling is also no accident, it is the consequence of a misguided project, deliberately and systematically uninformed by theory or research study. In the past decade and a half, politicians in a variety of Western countries who are concerned with education have launched continuing attacks on people they call 'educationists': the researchers and theorists of education. In Britain, from where I provide the bulk of my exemplary material, 'trendy theory' has been the brush with which these politicians have sought to tar all educational expertise in the form of research and reflection. Since a good deal of educational expertise might have warned against some of the wilder Government schemes, the accusation of 'trendy theory' was a way of stigmatizing that expertise, denying and dismissing accumulated knowledge as somehow unworthy of consideration. Theory is always easy to dismiss as impractical – a theorist like Albert Einstein was, after all, ridiculed for not being able to tie up his shoelaces; but in general the dismissal of expertise is not a terribly smart strategy, and so it has proved in the past decade and a half.

So in this chapter, I want to explore the much derided role that theoretical knowledge, and educational research specifically, can play in enhancing teacher professionalism. I want to argue that, in fact, theoretical bodies of knowledge, action research studies and reflective action – all of which take us beyond the uncritical and unreflective implementation of a practice defined by others – are central to the development of teacher professionalism and are also crucial in confirming the public's perception that teaching is a professional activity. A secondary concern of the chapter is to explore the degree to which theoretical knowledge and educational research, far from being useless and trendy, should be a major factor for any Government seriously interested in cost-effectiveness and efficient schooling.

Far from being a waste of money, as the very term 'trendy theory' implies, I shall argue that to ignore theory and educational research is to ignore some of the basic forms of expertise on which policy should be founded. The alternative is to make policy in the face of theoretical expertise and research knowledge, and the section on the British National Curriculum explores what happens when you turn your face against expertise in this manner. This has been a well documented episode and is chosen to exemplify the issue of the use or abuse of educational theory.

First, then, the relationship between educational research, reflective action, theoretical knowledge and the professional requirements of the teaching force. The important relationship to explore is between the pre-service and in-service needs of teachers and the continuing need for research and study of educational endeavour. Until recently in Britain these needs had existed in reasonable harmony. The university schools of education in Britain[1] developed after the McNair Report of 1944. McNair advised that universities should be involved in teacher education to ensure that teacher professionalism rose in the public's esteem. University involvement, it was argued, would make teaching 'become attractive to intelligent and cultured men and women' (McNair 1944).

University schools of education were given responsibility through their area training organizations for the provision of pre-service training not only in their own departments but in many 'training colleges'. It was these departments and schools of education that pioneered courses in the study of education as a significant contribution to the professional education of teachers. Courses were begun in educational psychology, in the history of education, in educational measurement, in experimental educational research, child development, and the philosophy of education. From the first, then, university schools of education established 'foundational' disciplines as the basis of educational study. In due course, sociology of education, curriculum studies and educational administration came to be added to the range of courses.

The courses of study taught in schools of education moved from a part-time to a largely full-time basis. Postgraduate training of teachers with degrees took place in year-long courses at university. Teachers often spent a year on secondment to university to complete a master's course.

> The standard of work achieved by the students was sound if academic. Classroom teachers were taught how to reflect on their teaching, on pupil learning, on the structure and organization of schools, to question educational assumptions and to understand how sexism and racism operated in the classroom.
> [McNair 1944]

These courses, then, enshrined the 'theoretical mission' of university study as well as practical preparation. But the theoretical mission should not be divorced from the assumption of practical effect. At its best, theory works back into informed and improved practice. Hence, 'some students used their new knowledge to render worthwhile changes in their teaching, to influence colleagues, to introduce new

---

[1] Variously known as Schools of Education, Departments of Education and Faculties of Education.

ways of examining, to improve the quality of discourse at staff meetings and the management and efficiency of teaching departments' (McNair 1944).

The presence of a diverse and informed student clientele provides enormous ongoing support to the work of educational scholarship in the university schools of education. At its best, in the university the work could move between theoretical preoccupation and practical predilection in ways that challenge both. But the two foci, theory and practice, have to be continually monitored and kept interlinked and 'in balance'.

The important point to grasp about the relationship between the varieties of theoretical knowledge and professional practice is that there is no inevitability about whether the relationship is good or bad. We know only too well what the view of theory is from many classrooms. A major factor in whether theoretical knowledge and educational research work symbiotically with professional practice is the civic mission and purposes of schooling in general. When those civilizing forces of civil cohesiveness are central as an objective in schooling, theory and practice tend to work well together. When, however, the agenda is more divisive, when 'there is no such thing as "society"' (Margaret Thatcher), when individual aggrandizement is promoted, it is not surprising that the cohesive forces which bind theoretical knowledge and professional practice together come under some strain. At times of divisiveness, theory is divorced from practice and can be presented as trendy. But such a claim is more a badge of civic abdication than of any intrinsic judgement on the nature of theory.

Certainly, histories of the relationship between theory and practice point to wide differentials in the nature of the gap between the two. The dichotomy, far from being wide and intractable, seems to be at least partially tractable, and highly variable over time. Simon (1985) examined the relationship between theory and practice in three periods, 1880–1900, 1920–1940 and 1940–1960. In the first and last periods he found 'a close relation between theory and practice'. For instance, in the period 1880–1900:

> For a whole concatenation of reasons, and from a variety of motives, it was thought that the masses should be educated, or at least schooled – and they were. This whole enterprise was, as it were, powered by an ideology – or theoretical stance – which emphasized the educability of the normal child, a view underpinned by advances in the field of psychology and physiology relating to human learning.
>
> [Simon 1985]

The point is that the potential for close relationship, or at the other extreme no relationship, between theory and practice depends on the aspirations of schooling, their social and political purposes in particular historical periods. Certainly in the 1960s and 1970s, new modalities of understanding and action sought to link theory and practice in generative ways: Stenhouse's critique of objectives modelling and development of the 'teacher as researcher' movement, Macdonald's work on 'democratic evaluation', Elliott's work on 'action research' and later, Schon's arguments for the reflective practitioner.

As we now know, in the period following 1979, 'trendy theory' became the monolithic enemy of those seeking to reform teacher education. An inevitable and continuous problem of balance, of how to reinstate and reinscribe a balance between theory and practice, was reinterpreted as a simple problem of location. As a result (like the narodniks in nineteenth-century Russia with their revolutionary 'back to the land' movement), we saw a 'back to the schools' movement develop. During the 1980s this fundamentalist programme made steady progress.

The initial period was one of incidental attrition. In the mid 1980s, money began to be redirected away from faculties of education. Social science research studentships rapidly decreased in number; so, therefore, did full-time masters and doctoral students. More significantly, in April 1987 the 'pool' of money by which local education authorities paid for the secondment of serving teachers was drained. Slowly the 'critical mass' of students required to keep up masters and research degrees disappeared. Deprived of this student clientele and associated research discourse, a good deal of faculty research also dried up, particularly as faculty now became more and more concerned with designing short school-based courses which were 'practical and relevant'.

In January 1992 attrition changed to outright redirection with Kenneth Clarke's new policy announced at the North of England Conference. Clarke announced that, at least in all secondary school subjects, henceforth 80 per cent of training would be moved from the university faculty of education schools to the secondary schools; this was later changed to 66 per cent of training time.

In Britain, I suspect the hasty embrace of the practical may lead to a collapse of the academic and theoretical mission of faculties of education. Logically this would seem to lead to the question being raised as to why such faculties, without substantial academic and theoretical missions, should any longer be located within the universities. This question may arise forcibly as universities seek to restructure themselves because of financial retrenchment. Because of the sharp pendulum swing away from too much theory towards 'practical relevance', the whole basis of the enterprise could be at risk. In short, in this time of change, we need to strike a new balance between theory, critique and practical matters. If we cannot strike such a balance, I believe the reflective and theoretical enterprise, broadly conceived, and educational research study generally, will begin to collapse. Far from this being solely a problem for educational scholars, I see it as a central problem for the teaching profession, for teaching is seen to be a profession because it is based on a set of research expertise and theoretical bodies of knowledge. This, incidentally, is true of all professions. Their claim to be professional is partially linked to the existence of theoretical bodies of expertise and knowledge. Once that is taken away, teaching can be presented as essentially a task for technicians and, once that is achieved, the capacity to essentially deprofessionalize teaching – thereby incidentally chopping away at working conditions, salaries and all the other perks of professionalism – will be enormously strengthened. Hence, the attack on trendy theory may also be an attack on teacher professionalism. So to revive and reinstate the relationship between research knowledge, theoretical knowledge and teachers' professional knowledge, is a crucial part of the task of enhancing teacher professionalism at this point in historical time.

Testing 'trendy theory': the case of the British National Curriculum

One way to examine whether 'trendy theory' is indeed as useless and empty as has often been implied is to look at some of the predictions which curriculum theorists made before the National Curriculum exercise was launched. In looking closely at what was said, we will be able to judge whether theorists were really in touch with what was likely to happen. We can see whether their advice would have been essentially wrong-headed and inaccurate for those articulating new policies, or whether it might not have been sensible to spend a little time and even money in funding educational research and theoretical studies before launching a massive new national initiative. The point to bear in mind about so much educational scholarship is that it is not written in a vacuum. Much of it grows from a very detailed understanding of the history, psychology, sociology and philosophy of education. It takes seriously the notion that we can learn something from history rather than just ignore it.

History in fact pointed to the likely response of teachers to dictated and uniform curriculum guidelines. Previous episodes such as payment by results in the period 1862 to 1895 led to 'a dismal failure' and to 'mechanical obedience' on the part of teachers and pupils. I argued that the then Government was 'reinventing the square wheel', and many other well-known curriculum theorists said the same.

Far from believing in 'the end of history' as some contemporary pundits do, curriculum theory believes that history can teach us profound lessons about the present and indeed the future. In an earlier article written in 1987 when the National Curriculum was first being formulated (it was introduced through the Education Reform Act of 1988), I said that in scrutinizing the arguments for Government intervention in school syllabuses, it was important to point to previous episodes when this was actually attempted. I then looked at the Lower Revised Code which was applied to elementary schools in 1862. From then until 1895 a major part of the grant received by each school was paid on the results of yearly examinations held by HM Inspectorate on a detailed syllabus, formulated by the Government and binding on all schools; thus it was similar to the linked pattern of National Curriculum and staged assessment.

In 1911 Edmond Holmes, a former Chief Inspector of Schools, wrote a devastating critique in his book *What Is and What Might Be*. First, he was concerned about the effects on teachers. On the official report of the yearly examination depended the reputation and financial prosperity of the school: 'The consequent pressure on the teacher to exert himself was well-nigh irresistible; and he had no choice but to transmit the pressure to his subordinates and his pupils. The result was that in those days the average school was a hive of industry' (Holmes 1928: 103).

So far so good, but 'it was also a hive of misdirected energy'. The impact on the teacher was passed on to the pupil:

> What the Department did to the teacher, it compelled him to do to the child. The teacher who is the slave of another's will cannot carry out his instructions except by making his pupils the slaves of his own will. The teacher who has been deprived by his superiors of freedom, initiative, and responsibility, cannot carry out his instructions except by depriving his pupils of the same vital qualities.
>
> [Holmes 1928: 104]

There might be two categories of objection to the argument so far. First, there would be those in Government who would argue that the 'minor' educational deficits Holmes describes are well worth accepting for the sake of finally establishing political control over the secondary school curriculum. Besides, they would say, the problems are merely short-term, a transitional psychological problem for teachers and taught. Secondly, there would be those who would question any similarities with the historical episode described – this is the twentieth century, and we are not discussing the re-establishment of the Lower Revised Code. In saying this, of course, they would be strictly correct. But as pointed out, the intention is merely to draw attention to the potential problems inherent in detailed Government intervention in school curricula. Here Holmes was clear about the essential *timelessness* of the problem. After all, he said:

> It is not only because mechanical obedience is fatal, in the long run, to mental and spiritual growth, that the regulation of elementary or any other grade of education by a uniform syllabus is to be deprecated. It is also because *a uniform syllabus is, in the nature of things, a bad syllabus*, and because the degree of its badness varies directly with the area of the sphere of educational activity that comes under its control.
>
> [Holmes 1928: 104–5]

In arguing that the problem was not specific to any historical period, but recurrent, Holmes was aware that the syllabuses issued by the department in the late nineteenth century were 'a grotesque blend of tragedy and farce'. But he warned that the problem was not merely to do with the passing inadequacies of the Government department, but was much more fundamental: 'Let us of the enlightened Twentieth Century try our hands at constructing a syllabus' and in so doing 'entrust the drafting of schemes of work in the various subjects to a committee of the wisest and most experienced educationalists in England' (Holmes 1928: 105).

Holmes was quite sure that the 'resultant syllabus would be a dismal failure' (Holmes 1928: 105).

In our contemporary schools, the imposition of a series of 'core' syllabuses defined by the previous Government with the eradication of the innovative, but deviant, Mode 3 teacher moderated examinations fall straight into the trap Holmes defines:

For in framing their schemes these wise and experienced educationalists would find themselves compelled to take account of the lowest rather than of the highest level of actual educational achievement. What is exceptional and experimental cannot possibly find a place in a syllabus which is to bind all schools and all teachers alike, and which must therefore be so framed that the least capable teacher, working under the least favourable conditions, may hope, when his pupils are examined on it, to achieve with decent industry a decent modicum of success. Under the control of a uniform syllabus, the schools which are now specialising and experimenting, and so giving a lead to the rest, would have to abandon whatever was interesting in their respective curricula, and fall into line with the average school; while, with the consequent lowering of the current *ideal* of efficiency, the level of the average school would steadily fall.

[Holmes 1928: 105–6]

The implications for the teacher of more uniform curricula were made abundantly clear:

The State, in prescribing a syllabus which was to be followed, in all subjects of instruction, by all the schools in the country, without regard to local or personal considerations, was guilty of one capital offence. It did all the thinking for the teacher. It told him in precise detail what he was to do each year in each 'Standard', how he was to handle each subject, and how far he was to go in it; what width of ground he was to cover; what amount of knowledge; what degree of accuracy was required for a 'pass'. In other words it provided him with his ideal, his general conceptions, his more immediate aims, his schemes of work . . .

[Holmes 1928: 103–4]

The growing impotence of the teacher was the expense of increased Government power – educational criteria sacrificed to political imperatives. Hence,

it was inevitable that in his endeavour to adapt his teaching to the type of question which his experience of the yearly examination led him to expect, he should gradually deliver himself, mind and soul, into the hands of the officials of the Department – the officials at Whitehall who framed the yearly syllabus, and the officials in the various districts who examined on it.

[Holmes 1928: 104]

When I last reflected on this historical episode and its lesson for contemporary curriculum reform, I concluded that too detailed a set of Government syllabuses would fail to carry the teaching force with it and would in the end contain the seeds of its own demise, leading to a collapse of teacher support and morale. One stream of Government policy in recent years had seen detailed intervention in school curricula and syllabuses as a way of arresting Britain's economic decline. As a diagnosis this policy seemed to be treating the wrong part of the patient's body – rather like putting an arm in plaster when the patient has tuberculosis.

On top of this the folly is compounded by the manner of treatment. Holmes's strictures against Government intervention warn us of the dangers inherent in the policy of uniform 'common core' curricula implemented through detailed syllabus guidelines. He warns of the inevitable 'lowest common denominator' element in such exercises. Learning from history and Holmes, I judged that

> in our state schools we have a wide variety of abilities, motivations and social characteristics. A starting point for achieving any common aims (or 'cores') with such a pupil clientele would be the acceptance that differential strategies will be required in the classroom. These strategies will not be amenable to uniform dictation from above for they depend on the kind of working knowledge of local and individual difference in which our teachers specialize.
>
> [Goodson 1981]

Since Holmes's early critiques, a very wide range of literature on educational change has confirmed the thrust of his critique of centralized prescriptions – the model of top-down dictation of change. This critique covers a wide range of countries – the work of Arthur Wirth and Ernest House on the inappropriateness of industrial models of change to the educational enterprise in the 1970s and 1980s developed this line of critique in the USA. Similarly in Canada, George Tomkins's studies of curriculum change over time pointed to the continuities and contradictions which stand against mandated change. And in Britain, Macdonald and Walker's critiques of teacher-proof innovations and the work of Lawrence Stenhouse, Jean Ruddock and John Elliott argued against simplistic prescriptive objectives planning and argued instead for process models and action research.

At the time of the launch of the National Curriculum, such 'trendy theory' insights and their warnings against too draconian a definition of what the teacher should do were widely ignored. Essentially, the then Government's view was that finely detailed syllabuses would define the teacher's task in ways that were beneficial for school students and, more broadly, the national interest. In its editorial at the launch of the National Curriculum, *The Times* applauded the definition of detailed curriculum guidelines and linked this with the assertion that 'in short, standards will rise'. This sort of optimism was in defiance of some of the historical and theoretical insights that might have been brought to bear on this issue.

In the event, the Government of the time chose not to spend a few hundred thousand pounds seeking advice from educational researchers and curriculum theorists, but to spend instead £750 million on a range of curriculum definition exercises. The belief was that by closely defining the teacher's delivery of the curriculum, 'standards would rise'.[2] So trendy theory and research expertise were ignored and

---

[2] The reference to 'standards would rise' comes from *The Times* editorial at the time. The editorial was headed 'A True Education Bill': 'Most important, a national curriculum accompanied by attainment targets and tests at key ages will ensure that a larger proportion of young people leave school literate, numerate and more broadly educated than they are now. Standards, in short, will rise. That is because teachers will have a clearer idea of what is expected of them' (*The Times*, 21 November 1987).

gut instincts were followed. It was not a case of competing expertises when the National Curriculum was launched, but of ignoring existing research and theoretical expertise and pushing ahead in denial and defiance of it. To ignore expertise, whether you stigmatize it as trendy theory or not, is not a very smart move; this is being clearly indicated by the fate of the National Curriculum exercise.

This is not the place to discuss all of the various battles in the different subject committees or the various boycotts when teacher groups reacted in the way that history fairly clearly indicated they might. But a few culminating comments about the National Curriculum will show that my own jaundiced view about the neglect of theory is not a singular or eccentric one. The rapid learning curve of people watching the National Curriculum is indicated by the comparison of the original *Times* editorial, which assumed that the close definition of syllabuses would immediately lead to rising standards, with the astonishing panicky article in *The Times* at the time of the teachers' boycott, where the then Government is accused of gross incompetence for trying to define the curriculum and its assessment in too close and draconian a way. A few years is a very short curve. Unfortunately, £750 million was spent during the learning curve when a fairly basic perusal of theory and expertise would have indicated clearly what the pitfalls would be.

> Sir Ron Dearing finally buried the Baker legislation and unveiled a national curriculum remarkably similar to that which existed before Baker began to meddle . . .
> The whole sorry exercise has wasted in the region of £750 million, driven thousands of teachers into early retirement and brought unhappiness and disruption to home and school.
>
> [*Observer* 1994]

With regard to the question of stress, the recent work of Professor Cary Cooper has shown quite dramatically how stress among teachers has risen since the National Curriculum was unveiled. Cooper argues that 'lack of control induces stress – losing control, particularly so' (Cooper 1994). The National Curriculum is then seen as the major agency for teachers' sense of losing control and for the dramatic increase in stress levels, the collapse of teacher morale and the flood of early retirements that have been noted.

> In teaching, 'the nature of the job has totally changed', says Dr Cooper, who has recently conducted a national study of 1,800 teachers. 'They have had the imposition of the national curriculum, assessment and local financial management of schools. A teacher now aged 40 to 45 went in expecting a lot of autonomy in the job. Control has now been taken away.'
>
> [Bosely 1994]

Lest it be thought that these reports have been drawn selectively from newspapers sympathetic to my critical view, the *Daily Telegraph*'s conclusion about the National Curriculum is revealing.

In the end, it was the complex and time consuming system of assessment devised by yet another working crew that led to the national teachers' boycott and the collapse of the entire structure . . .

Evidence from Her Majesty's Inspectors suggest that the principal gains are a beefing up of the primary curriculum, the introduction of design and technology, and a requirement that all pupils should at least have a nodding acquaintance with a modern foreign language . . .

Whether that could have been achieved more simply and cheaply was not a question Mrs Sheppard was prepared to discuss.

[*Daily Telegraph* 1994]

These media commentators have begun to ask why, indeed, the previous Government ignored theory and history and educational research when it embarked upon the National Curriculum. For example, *The Times* was euphoric at the prospects of the National Curriculum but became greatly disillusioned.

The outgoing chairman of the National Curriculum Council, David Pascall, moans in *The Times Educational Supplement* that teachers 'seem to be teaching the test'. What did he and Mr Patton expect? If they impose upon teachers a detailed curriculum and testing regime, and tell them they will be paid and their schools judged on the outcome, the schools will teach the test. This is no surprise, it happened when government last tried payment by results in the 19th century. Is history not studied in the Education Department?

[*The Times* 1993]

Another report commented:

The key message Sir Ron delivered on Thursday [this is in November] was that professional responsibility is to be handed back to the teachers within a broad framework, they will decide what goes on in the classroom. This is common sense; it is what we train them, and pay them to do. Good teachers are driven by their imagination, their knowledge, their love of the subject. We want more individuality and eccentricity in the classroom, not less. But like actors, artists and other creative people, teachers need constant ego massage – it is difficult to perform well when subjected to constant abuse.

So along with the other quality newspapers, *The Times* and the *Daily Telegraph* concluded that the major problem in the whole National Curriculum exercise was that the then Government refused to listen to research expertise, to historical and theoretical studies and the lessons they could teach. The result of stigmatizing this previous expertise as 'trendy theory' has been a cost of £750 million for an exercise which eventually and tragically demonstrated what the original 'trendy' theorists were so desperately trying to indicate was likely to happen all along. This should serve as a strong warning to the new and future Governments not to ignore and stigmatize theory in this way.

Empirical work on the National Curriculum has substantiated the critiques made by 'trendy theorists'. A wide survey of teachers interviewed by Helsby and

McCulloch showed how the government onslaught of edicts and initiatives demolished planning and professionalism. In their study they concluded:

> The introduction of a centralized and prescriptive National Curriculum appears to have weakened their professional confidence, lowered morale and left them uncertain both of their ability to cope and of their right to take major curriculum decisions. These findings are consistent with the view of increased State control of the curriculum undermining teacher professionalism.

In other countries, the same pattern has emerged. Robertson's investigation into contemporary restructuring of teachers' work in Australia and elsewhere also makes reference to 'a new professionalism', but her own use of the term is decidedly ironic.

> There is little scope in the promise of professionalism to wrest a degree of autonomy because the crucial margin for determination that is ideological control has been unceremoniously split from teachers' work and placed in the firm hands of administrators, politicians and transnational capital. The margin of indetermination is now located at the level of decisions to meet the system specified outcomes, rather than at the point of judgement about what might constitute an adequate framing of knowledge. Gains to teachers are thus largely illusory. Teachers will be weighed down by the pressure of (self) management, time constraints, larger classes and the management of other workers. What flows from this is a depersonalized authority, an outcome teachers have confused with professionalism. Teachers have not been provided or promised an opportunity to negotiate the changing shape of their work. Rather, their work has increasingly been moulded by economic imperative and expediency, and is the outcome of the state's need to establish the new conditions for accumulation.

The fate of the trendy theorist has been synonymous with the fate of the classroom teacher. But clearly the time has come for the pendulum to swing back. It is time to bring the teachers back into the fold and with them, educational researchers and theorists who seek to support teachers' professional knowledge. How might this project be pursued? How might theory and practice be harmonized in productive ways?

Developing teacher-centred theory

Whilst I have argued that theory, even trendy theory, has much to offer, I would be the first to agree that theory can be improved. The particular problem that should now concern us is how to maintain, revive and establish a collaborative and theoretical mission within a new, more field-based and school-based terrain, and in so doing bring new strength and vigour to collaborative research and theory work with teachers. As well as developing the ideas and theories already laid out in the substantial literature on teacher–teacher collegiality and collaboration – a very important directional shift – I believe this means looking closely at the potential collaboration between teachers and externally located researchers in faculties of education. I believe the best mechanism for improving practice is if teachers, in an ongoing way, research and reflect upon their own practice. This may not seem as self-evident as stated: many great teachers would say 'why the hell should I need research, I can teach already'.

Teachers I have studied over the years have one thing in common. Whilst they may say they are uninterested in research, nevertheless in their own lives and in their teaching they constantly reflect upon and refine their practice. They try new things, work at what is not working well, and generally think through the problems that face them. In other words, they research their own practice. Now it could be said that since they do this and are great teachers, obviously there is no place for externally located researchers to aid their ongoing research. But this still leaves a great percentage who are not great teachers looking for help. For such lesser mortals (including myself), I believe a collaborative relationship which focuses on researching our own 'life and work' is the most hopeful avenue for enhanced professional development.

What might this collaborative relationship between teachers and externally located researchers in faculties of education look like? I want to argue that a narrow focus on 'practice' in collaborating on research, a panacea that is politically popular at the moment, will not take us too far. This is for two reasons: (1) practice is a good deal more than the technical things we do in classrooms – it relates to who we are, to our whole approach to life. Here I might quote C. Wright Mills talking about scholars, but it is as relevant to any member of the community. He said: 'the most admirable thinkers within the scholarly community . . . do not split their work from their lives. They seem to take both too seriously to allow such disassociation and they want to use each for the enrichment of others'; (2) the interactive practices of our classrooms are subject to constant change. Often in the form of new Government guidelines like the National Curriculum, these initiatives outside the classroom, what I call preactive actions, set crucial parameters for interactive classroom practice. Preactive action effects interactive possibilities. In their collaborative research, teachers as researchers and external researchers need to focus on both the preactive and the interactive. What this means, in short, is that we need to look at the full context in which teachers' practice is negotiated, not just at the technical implementation of certain phenomena within the classroom. If we stay with the latter definition, our research is inevitably going to involve the mere implementation of initiatives which are generated elsewhere. This reduces the involvement and commitment of everyone involved.

The area of inquiry I want to sketch out would focus on the teacher's work and practice in the full context of the teacher's life.

The project I am recommending is essentially one of reconceptualizing educational research so as to ensure that teachers' voices are heard, heard loudly, heard articulately. In this respect the most hopeful way forward is, I think, to build upon notions of the 'self-monitoring teacher', 'the teacher as researcher', the teacher as 'extended professional'. For instance, in the early 1970s at the Centre for Applied Research in Education at the University of East Anglia in England, a good deal of work was conducted into how to operationalize this concept. Perhaps the most interesting developments were within the Ford Teaching Project conducted by John Elliott and Clem Adelman in the period 1973–75. They sought to rehabilitate the 'action-research' mode pioneered by Kurt Lewin in the post-war period. In the interim period educational action research had fallen into decline. Carr and Kemmis (1986), who have done a good deal to extend and popularize the concept, give a number of reasons for the resurgence of action-research:

> First, there was the demand from within an increasingly professionalized teacher force for a research role, based on the notion of the extended professional investigating his or her own practice. Second, there was the perceived irrelevance to the concerns of these practitioners of much contemporary educational research. Third, there had been a revival of interest in 'the practical' in curriculum, following the work of Schwab and others on 'practical deliberation'. Fourth, action research was assisted by the rise of the 'new wave' methods in educational research and evaluation with their emphasis on participants' perspectives and categories in shaping educational practices and situations. These methods place the practitioners at centre stage in the educational research process and recognize the crucial significance of actors' understandings in shaping educational action. From the role of critical informant helping an 'outsider' researcher, it is but a short step for the practitioner to become a self-critical researcher into her or his own practice. Fifth, the accountability movement galvanized and politicized practitioners. In response to the accountability movement, practitioners have adopted the self-monitoring role as a proper means of justifying practice and generating sensitive critiques of the working conditions in which their practice is conducted. Sixth, there was increasing solidarity in the teaching profession in response to the public criticism which has accompanied the post-expansion educational politics of the 1970s and 1980s; this, too, has prompted the organization of support networks of concerned professionals interested in the continuing developments of education even though the expansionist tide has turned. And, finally, there is the increased awareness of action research itself, which is perceived as providing an understandable and workable approach to the improvement of practice through critical self-reflection.

The focus of action-research has, however, tended to be very practice-oriented. In introducing a survey of action-research, for instance, Carr and Kemmis (1986) note: 'A range of practices have been studied by educational action-researchers and some examples may suffice to show how they have used action research to improve their practices, their understandings of these practices, and the situations in which they work.'

Not surprisingly, with the notion of an extended professional in mind, workers have 'used action-research to improve their practice'. But it is ever more important to develop a holistic base for teacher professional knowledge, looking at the teacher's life and work in a more general perspective.

Taking the 'teacher as researcher' and 'action-research' as expressing defensible value positions and viable starting points, I want to argue for a broadened sense of purpose, moving from a sole focus on practice to develop theory and research knowledge about the full range of the teacher's working life.

Much of the emerging study in this area indicates that this focus allows a rich flow of dialogue and data. Moreover, the focus may (and I stress may) allow teachers greater authority and control in collaborative research than has often appeared to be the case with practice-oriented study. What I am asserting here is that, particularly in the world of teacher development, the central ingredient so far missing is *teachers' voices*. Primarily the focus has been on the teacher's practice, almost the teacher *as* practice. What is needed is a focus that listens above all to the person at whom 'development' is aimed. This means that strategies should be developed which facilitate, maximize and in a real sense legitimate teachers' voices. In short, for practical theory, university schools of education have important symbolic as well as strategic value. Let me end by quoting Philip Taylor, England's first holder of a Chair in Curriculum Studies: 'any profession whose essential theoretical and practical knowledge does not have a high place in universities and other institutions of higher education, must count itself deprived and in the long run, be diminished in status' (Taylor 1987). We should beware of the attack on theory; besides being an attack on educational theorists and researchers, it can so easily become an attack on the status and significance of teaching as a profession.

This result should be closely considered by those trying to link educational research and practice and to promote only that research which feeds directly into practice. In this case I agree with Tony Edwards (1996), who doubts: 'the sense of treating as useful only research targeted directly at classroom practice; as though an understanding of the wider contexts of learning was not a vital component of professional knowledge'.

In reflecting on the money spent on the implementation of the National Curriculum and the abject refusal to fund new research or even scrutinize existing research, the notion of 'mad curriculum disease' is relevant. The refusal to fund research into mad cow disease led to analogous if more expensive results. So I share Edwards's (1996) beliefs and hopes:

> I certainly hope that the ESRC and Charities continue to fund research which is long term, driven by curiosity, and not bound by an obligation to be immediately useful. But even research dedicated to improving practice requires the freedom to contest orthodoxies, to publish politically unconventional findings and where the evidence justifies it, to complicate (over) simple solutions.

The issue of political control over research is of central importance. By arguing for educational research to be primarily practice-driven, many commentators fail to address this point. For since 'practice' can be politically and socially prescribed, practice-driven research opens a further door to political control. Making educational research and theory conform to short-term political needs is unlikely to aid the long-term health of the educational system.

References

Bosely, S. (1994) Old disease made acute by family and job changes, *The Guardian*, 17 November, p. 3.

Carr, W. and Kemmis, S. (1986) *Becoming Critical: Education Knowledge and Action Research*. London, New York and Philadelphia: Falmer Press.

Cooper, C. (1994) *The Guardian*, 18 November.

Daily Telegraph (1994) *Daily Telegraph*, 11 November.

Edwards, T. (1996) The research base of effective teacher education. *Research Intelligence*, July, pp. 10–11.

Goodson, I. (1981) Re-inventing the square wheel. *Times Educational Supplement*, 17 April, p. 17.

Helsby, G. and McCulloch, G. (1993) The character of the new National Curriculum. Paper presented at the Spencer Hall Conference, Mimeo, 12–14 September.

Holmes, E. (1928) *What Is and What Might Be*. London: Constable.

Hutton, W. (1994) *The Guardian*, 13 June, p. 5.

McNair Report of 1944 quoted in P. Taylor (1987) Whiff of defeat in school scandal, *The Times Higher Education Supplement*, 13 November, p. 14.

Observer (1994) *The Observer*, 15 November, p. 28.

Robertson, S. (1993) Towards a new professionalism. Paper presented at the Spencer Hall Conference, Mimeo, 12–14 September.

Simon, B. (1985) *Does Education Matter?* London: Lawrence and Wishart.

Taylor, P. (1987) Whiff of defeat in schools scandal, *The Times Higher Education Supplement*, 13 November, p. 14.

The Times (1993) *The Times*, 12 May, p. 14.

4 TEACHERS IN THE TWENTY-FIRST CENTURY: TIME TO RENEW THE VISION

Christopher Day

For many teachers, the past 20 years have been years of survival rather than development. As social and economic change has placed new demands upon and created new expectations from schools, hardly a year has passed without some reform being mooted, negotiated or imposed in the name of raising standards (appraisal, inspection), increasing 'user' participation (open enrolment, local financial management) and pupil entitlement (a national curriculum). Traditional relationships between local education authorities and schools have been dismembered as Governments have pursued simultaneously a 'loose tight' centralization (of teachers' pay and conditions of service, curriculum control, testing and school inspections) and decentralization (delegating school budgets, school management planning and control of management of schools to governing bodies). Though the nature of Government intervention in England and Wales has not always mirrored that of other countries, the universal effects have been similar. Teachers have had to bear an increased workload; and their energy levels and motivation remain at best 'frayed around the edges' as pressures of increased class sizes, teacher redundancies and teacher shortages grow.

There has been little time to reflect. The changing vocabulary of 'initial teacher training' (rather than education), 'training days', 'delivery' of teaching, 'inspection', 'performance appraisal' and 'competency' together with increased stress levels bears testimony to the changing operational definition of professionalism.

Many educational researchers themselves have become part of policy implementation as they struggle to find ways in which schools and teachers can become more 'effective', whilst others seek to mediate the unhelpful introduction of decontextualized league tables by results and over-simplified forms of student assessment.

Bound and gagged in the confines of 'doing their best' in what are often adverse circumstances; with self-esteem battered by the insistent haranguing of those in high office who might be expected to have some empathy if not sympathy rather than engaging in public denigration, and who should know that constant measurement and assessment without the equivalent support will do little to encourage the continuing motivation and commitment so essential to good teaching; it is little wonder that many teachers have lost sight of why they came into teaching in the first place – to make a difference in the lives of students.

Yet I would predict that teachers in the twenty-first century will become more, rather than less, important to society, and that their contributions to the socio-economic health of nations will become more valued. It is difficult to predict the future, and at times like this it is not easy to make this kind of statement without worrying that one will be accused of being idealistic or hopelessly out of touch with the real world. The kind of scenario in the year 2000 which might exist, without change of direction, is one in which teachers will be working in increasingly dilapidated schools, with larger classes and resources inadequate for stimulating and challenging their pupils. Their salaries will be locally negotiated and performance-rated against pre-specified behavioural competences. School standards will be policed by Ofsted. Teachers emerging from training will be technically proficient and able to deliver the curriculum efficiently, and professional development will be defined by activities directly related to knowledge and skills updating. Many teachers will be on fixed-term contracts. Teaching will be just a job. It will not attract the best minds and spirits. Students will be short-changed. The long-term health of the nation will continue to be sacrificed on the altar of short-term results.

Yet there are reasons for believing that if Governments act upon the growing international as well as national recognition of the importance of lifelong learning for all, teachers will have a central part to play. So what I want to present here is a vision of what *might* be. There have been too many maps to follow over the past ten years and not enough vision. Maps plot that which exists. Visions create that which does not yet exist, the reasons for travelling, and the destination which will provide the best reward for the journey. Yet visions must take account of the world in which we live. In the case of teachers, this means taking account of the changes in the social, economic and technological world and the world of the child. I intend to focus upon these now as a means of identifying the changing role and crucial importance of the teacher in the twenty-first century.

The changing student: where students are coming from

We need, first, to understand children within the context of the complexities of modern family life . . . Parenting presents a considerable challenge, particularly as non-traditional family patterns continue to grow. Looking to the future, Gibson (1994) has predicted that, 'by the first decade of the new century, some 45 per cent of children will, if present trends continue, have experienced some form or other of a non-conjugal household structure by the time they reach sixteen years of age ... The need to support parents is incontrovertible.'

[Walker 1995]

The first findings from the ESRC's *British Household Panel Study* (Buck *et al.* 1994) provide a unique insight into how people's lives have changed in the 1990s. For example:

▶ the standard household of husband, wife and children is now a minority formation (40 per cent), and there has been a substantial increase in the proportion of single-parent households (10 per cent) and people who live alone (11 per cent);
▶ the growth in women's employment continues (70 per cent of 30-year-olds with children now have jobs);
▶ the growth in men's self-employment continues (from 6 per cent to 12 per cent over the past 20 years).

The report by the Rowntree Foundation (Cockett and Tripp 1994) provides further interesting insights into the experiences which many students bring with them into the classroom. In England and Wales 31 per cent of children are now born outside marriage. Forty per cent of marriages entailed a remarriage for one partner, and such marriages carry a greater risk of breakdown. Parents' own conflicts and distress may mean that they are less likely to be able to support their children emotionally. Children who experience family disruption are more likely to suffer social, educational and health problems than a comparable sample whose families remain intact (Cockett and Tripp 1994).

Lone parents constitute 19 per cent, or one in five of all families. They tend to be poorer, and poverty creates additional stresses. One-third of children in the UK as a whole live in families with an income under half the national income; a fifth live on income support. Children of lone parents are particularly at risk of poverty, because so frequently in the UK, parents are unable to find employment which covers the cost of childcare. Poverty affects the quality of childcare in the home as well, as the provision of basic physical needs – food, clothing, healthcare, stress, debts, poor housing, isolation in communities, lack of accessible social amenities – all combine to make supportive parenting extremely difficult.

The UK has one of the lowest levels of investment in public housing in Europe. There is a marked shortage of affordable accommodation, and rent and housing needs have been exacerbated by unemployment and repossession of homes in owner-occupation.

Differences in families are not only due to poverty. Rich or poor, many children are, in effect, 'only children'. Mothers (approximately 60 per cent of them) are back at work, full- or part-time, about one year after the child's birth.

Children may seem to be more sophisticated in some respects, especially in relation to technology, but there are now fewer opportunities for activities such as outdoor play with peers. Whilst they may be heavier and larger than a few generations earlier and clearly more physically mature, they may also be more vulnerable.

Certainly, they will often have surprisingly sedentary lives, and obesity among children has increased. Many live in flats, houses, or circumstances where, for their own safety, they have to be confined indoors. They watch considerable amounts of TV and video, often unsupervised and alone. We still do not know the long-term effects on young children of exposure to TV and video violence.

Many children have little experience of physical or social play – perhaps no knowledge of the richness of nursery rhymes and singing games, perhaps little chance to share with and care for their peers, possibly little opportunity to register autonomy and pride in their own achievements. Difficulties in later social adjustment may well be reflected in *lack of appropriate early provision for all children.* Teachers of school-age children experience a higher incidence of behaviour difficulties. Some children lack motivation, self-esteem and self-confidence. The vulnerable child need not necessarily come from an impoverished financial background – all children are vulnerable. All depend upon the quality of their early experience in home and school; such experiences are crucial.

More than ever, then, schools will need to represent a secure place for students; and teachers, whatever their specialism or phase, will need to have as a priority the ability to mediate between the different and often conflicting messages which they receive.

It has been worth visiting, briefly, the kinds of experience that students are likely to bring with them into school – with which teachers will have to work if they are to gain the commitment and motivation which underpins effective learning – and the kind of world which they are likely to enter. If nothing else this will remind those policymakers and others at a distance from the crowded and not always predictable world of most poorly resourced schools and classrooms that teaching, at its heart, needs to be based upon a holistic understanding of the taught, both collectively and individually (the operationalization of the principle of differentiation). Teachers are, after all, responsible for meeting the spiritual, cultural, moral, mental and physical development needs of children, and for preparing them for the opportunities, responsibilities and experiences of adult life.

The changing world: where students are going to

Schools are not only places within which teachers have responsibilities for mediating values; they also exist within socio-economic contexts and contribute to them. It is therefore important to vision-forming that these contexts are considered, for they too inform the teachers' role.

There is, according to the International Labour Organization, a higher proportion of people unemployed in the world than at any time since the 1930s. Some 30 per cent, or 820 million people, are either unemployed or underemployed' (McRae 1995). McRae reported that the annual report of the International Labour Organization, a United Nations agency, suggests that part of the problem in Europe is that international market pressures are forcing rapid changes in the structure of industrial economies which are now having to move from producing 'low value-added goods and services into high-technology and high-quality service industries'. In the USA, for example, one effect has been 'to displace low-skill workers and increase the demands for highly skilled ones'. The analyst concludes (McRae 1995) that if this trend is followed in Europe:

> the only way we can sustain, or even improve, the relatively high living standards that most people in the developed world enjoy is if we are educated, trained and motivated to produce the high quality goods and services that justify such standards.

The need for more highly-educated, motivated employees who are able to use more autonomy in applying skills in combination with flexible technology and work processes to produce more per worker is recognized, too, in the USA, where the move from the specialist to the adaptable generalist is well under way:

> Employers want employees with solid academic basics, but they want the applied versions of the three Rs. Applied reading, writing, and mathematics are substantially different from the versions taught in schools. In addition, employers want a set of behavioural skills that are not taught at all in traditional academic curricula, such as problem solving, communication skills, interpersonal skills and leadership.
>
> [Carnevale 1994]

According to research undertaken by the Institute of Employment in the UK, 'by the year 2000, 70 per cent of all jobs in Europe will require people with professional skill – those with A levels and above. Only 30 per cent of jobs will require skills at a level below that'. The 70–30 per cent ratio is 'broadly a reversal of the immediate post-war ratio of employment'. Toombs (1994) goes on to suggest that, until recently, we have excelled in our education system at ensuring that about 30 per cent of our young people were well qualified.

We are also part of a European Union where 'more than 10 per cent of the workforce is without a job, 50 per cent higher than jobless rates in the US and almost five times higher than in Japan . . . In 1992 the EC ran a trade deficit of $90 billion with the rest of the world, three times the 1985–90 average' (Naisbitt 1994: 303).

Evidence of the UK's lack of competitiveness in the global economy was provided by Howard Davies, Director of the CBI, at the North of England Conference in 1993:

> in terms of world competitiveness, the 1992 report of the World Economic Forum placed Britain thirteenth out of 22 OECD countries. We were twentieth out of 22 countries for the quality of our people skills. We have fewer university graduates as a percentage of the population – some 23 per cent in the US, 13 per cent in Japan, and 9 per cent here.

In what has been described as one of the most forward-looking of the 1980s' best books, *The Age of Unreason* (1989), Charles Handy wrote of discontinuous rather than continuous change. He predicted that in the next century, companies will be 'reluctant to guarantee careers for life to everyone ... More contracts will be for fixed periods of years, more appointments will be tied to particular roles or jobs with no guarantee of further promotion' (Handy 1989: 125).

He goes on to suggest that:

> Careers will therefore become more variegated. In larger companies there will still be opportunity for variety and advancement, but as these companies get more federal more decisions will be left to the separate parts with the centre being left with a brokerage and counselling role. It will increasingly be the individual's responsibility to make sure that the opportunities on offer add up to a sensible career path ... Education in those circumstances becomes an investment, wide experience an asset provided that it is wide and not shallow ...
>
> [Handy 1989: 127]

It is not surprising, then, that Government has placed increasing emphasis over the past decade on creating job training schemes, and on attempting to make the curriculum of secondary schools and further and higher education more vocationally oriented, in more and more desperate attempts to increase the nation's ability to compete. Sadly, it has failed to take note of the real implications of economic change for the school curriculum, and has created a content-driven curriculum when one which is process-driven is clearly demanded.

The telecommunications revolution

There is a third strand to be visited briefly if we are to have a clear view of life in the twenty-first century. Both outside and inside school, if we are to believe what we are told, there will be a continuing exponential expansion of telecommunications. This information technology will provide students – indeed all of us – with more opportunities to learn through CD-ROMs, virtual reality and interactive technologies which will enable people from different parts of the world to talk to each other simultaneously, to 'surf' the Internet, to cruise the information superhighway. There can, then, be no doubt that:

> the telecommunications revolution will enlarge the role of the individual with more access to information, greater speed in execution, and greater ability to communicate to anyone or to greater numbers anywhere, anytime. All trends are in the direction of making the smallest player in the global economy more and more powerful.
>
> [Naisbitt 1994: 357]

Looking ahead: students as lifelong learners

One certainty, then, that we may predict for the twenty-first century is that times will not become more settled. The sense of 'fragmentation, breakdown and loss of meaning which pervades post-modern cultures' (Beare and Slaughter 1993: 15) is likely to continue. In a context of 'compulsive technological dynamism, competitive individualism and a radical loss of meaning and purpose, schools are in an impossible position, standing as they do at the crucial interface between past and future, charged both with the conservation of culture and with its radical renewal' (Beare and Slaughter 1993: 15).

In British Columbia, Canada, the Sullivan Commission, in the 'Year 2000 Framework Learning' report, recognized that society is changing and that the structure of the economy is shifting from being 'primarily resource-based to becoming a mixed economy' with increasing emphasis on the information and service sectors. It declared that:

> In view of the new social and economic realities, *all* students, regardless of their immediate plans following school, will need to develop a flexibility and versatility undreamed of by previous generations. Increasingly, they will need to be able to employ critical and creative thinking skills to solve problems and make decisions, to be technologically literate as well as literate in the traditional sense, and to be good communicators. Equally, they will need to have well developed interpersonal skills and be able to work cooperatively with others. Finally, they will need to be lifelong learners.
>
> [Ministry of Education 1991: 2]

This could equally have been written in Australia or in any European country. It is clear where the emphasis in schooling must be, and it is equally clear that the quality of teachers and their teaching will be vital if they are to contribute to the endeavour of lifelong learning for the twenty-first century which is so regularly espoused by Government and business as being essential.

There is no doubt that 'lifelong learning for all' will be an established part of everyone's agenda for the twenty-first century. The EU declared 1996 the 'Year of Lifelong Learning'; UNESCO will enter the third millennium with a new inter-disciplinary project, 'Learning Without Frontiers', in which the establishment of a culture of learning is the main focus. In the words of its Director General, Dr Frederico Mayor:

> the purpose of learning can no longer be regarded as no more than an initial preparation for the remainder of one's life. Learning in the twenty-first century will be a continuous requirement. It will be the responsibility of societies to provide an environment, free of any barriers, in which individuals and social entities alike can satisfy their learning needs.

In England, the authors of 'Learning to Succeed', the Report of the National Commission on Education, suggested that:

> Perhaps the most critical task of all in the years ahead is to persuade a greater number of men and women that learning is for them, that it can improve their personal lives and that there are opportunities for them to seize. The goal in

the end is to create a learning culture, a society in which learning is the norm and the question people ask when the possibility of education or training arises for them is not, 'why should I?' but 'why shouldn't I?'

[NCE 1993: 332]

This theme is being echoed across the world in statements by Governments, industrialists and educationalists alike.

The findings of the First Global Conference on Lifelong Learning (1994) also point the way forward, in a context in which 'in the twenty-first century those individuals who do not practise lifelong learning will not find work; those organisations which do not become learning organisations will not survive . . .'. The 500 people drawn from 50 nations attending this conference were clear that the development of companies, schools, colleges and universities will be essential rather than desirable, if they are to survive; that 'the challenge for individuals is to achieve and maintain their own employability through lifelong learning'; that 'the key to successful learning is motivation', which 'will not be achieved by means of tight centralised control'. The bad news is that, according to the European Round Table of Industrialists' report on lifelong learning, at present *education has the lowest level of capital investment of any major industry today'*.

Investing in teachers

The paradox of lifelong learning is that it requires people to start right from their earliest years at school, and for a love of learning to be nurtured by their teachers – so often a feature in descriptions by adults of their 'best teachers' who are completely dedicated to the job, have a 'passion for the excitement of the intellectual life' and whose 'greatest satisfaction' is to share it with their students. As with children, so with teachers the key to successful learning is motivation, which cannot be achieved by means of tight centralized control. Personal commitment and involvement are likely to be limited when teachers must follow dictums devised by others (Rubin 1989).

Getting professional development right: starting with self-esteem

In one respect Chris Woodhead the Head of Ofsted (Office for Standards in Education) has got it right. Teachers do have to be open-minded, more sceptical of the received wisdom (of the National Curriculum, virtues of appraisal and Ofsted inspection criteria), more flexible and probing. We must, as he says, turn from preoccupation with recent legislation to take on the priority issue: 'Our vision of the educational good, our expectations of what children can and should achieve and the teaching methods we use as we seek to initiate our pupils into the best that has been thought and said' (Hackett 1995).

However, he has also got it badly wrong, for he has chosen to deliver his message in ways which implicitly deny the complexity of the job of teaching and the importance of context, and which fail to take account of the need to build rather than destroy the self-esteem of a profession which, judging by the growing rate of retirements through ill health (almost doubled in the past decade), needs informed, caring support rather than politically inspired criticism: 'You have to believe, in this business, that you are making things better and moving things on. If that particular spark is not there – if something happens that makes you think things are going the opposite way – it can be a very destroying occupation' (Clarke 1995).

Beyond competence: teaching skills are not enough

Recently, it has been argued that improving teachers' skills is the only way to bring about the better standards of learning the nation requires, that the time has come to 'shift the focus of policy from the structure and regulation of education, to teaching and learning itself', so that teachers might be supported in 'acquiring and maintaining the most refined, advanced skills in pedagogy' (Barber 1994b). Whilst no one could fail to support this sensible plea, to focus upon developing teaching methods alone and to promote one over another, is to miss the point of professional development. A study of six cohorts of adults aged from 22 to 74, published in 1994 by the Adult Literacy and Basic Skills Unit, shows that the 1960s 'child-centred' taught pupils were as good at reading and arithmetic as the so-called 'traditionally' taught pupils of the 1950s; and the Gallup sample of 3000 adults and 2800 assessments showed, disturbingly, that 'the 22–24-year-olds, who left school between 1988 and 1990 and were the most recently educated, were significantly worse at solving more advanced mathematical problems than those 10 or 20 years older'.

It was only the final paragraph of the article which touched the heart of the matter, when Michael Barber wrote that policy 'should be designed to cherish and restore the sense of idealism which is at the core of all good teaching'. As education-alists we need to remind ourselves that personal mastery goes beyond competence and skills, and that maintaining and developing individual and collective vision *is simply not possible without the continuing career-long committed professionalism of teachers*.

Experts in learning: continuing professional development

In Luxembourg recently, ETUCE, the European Assembly of Teacher Trade Unions which includes representatives from the National Union of Teachers (NUT), Association of Teachers and Lecturers (ATL), National Association of Teachers in Further and Higher Education (NATFHE) and National Association of Schoolmasters/Union of Women Teachers (NAS/UWT), found that teachers 'play a key role not only in the transmission of culture but in preparing students for a *future where continuous change is a certainty*' (7.2); that 'Initial teacher education can be no more than a preliminary to the professional development required both for specific career routes within teaching and for the continuous development required of a professional' (7.4); and that 'Static or linear conceptions of teacher education must be replaced by a holistic understanding of the inter-relatedness of teachers' personal and professional development with research and development, school improvement and the changing social and political aspirations for the education service and by an appreciation that a dynamic system will challenge existing organisational structures and power bases and require responsiveness to the needs of the practitioners' (7.12) (ETUCE 1994).

The National Commission on Education envisages teachers in the twenty-first century as experts in effective learning

> with the capacity to think deeply about educational aims and values, and thereby critically about educational programmes . . . willing to motivate and encourage each and every pupil, assess progress and learning needs in their widest sense, even when this involves them in areas outside formal education.
>
> [NCE 1993: 196–7]

If these visions are to be realized, opportunities for continuing professional development must be available, and fully resourced, which recognize that, for teachers as for students and other adults of the twenty-first century, learning is a lifelong business. *Investing in education means investing in the continuing professional development of teachers.* All students are entitled, as Sir Clauser Moser stated at the 1993 North of England Conference, 'to be taught by good teachers qualified to teach the subject in question; and the success, quality and enjoyment of what goes on in schools depends above all on the heads and teaching staff'. Yet so far, the bulk of in-service provision in recent years has focused upon 'keeping teachers updated about recent reforms, in particular the curriculum', and has '*hindered* personal development and the continuing development of teaching practices and strategies' (NCE 1993: 219). Conditions of schooling continue to ensure that teachers have insufficient time to reflect on their purposes and practice. Learning does not stop when the 'expert' stage is reached – indeed, expertise may be seen as a potentially limiting state. As for students, these opportunities must be based upon principles of differentiation, coherence, continuity and progression, and balance. Need must be recognized as being at times oriented towards personal development, at times towards longer-term intellectual and reflective development, at times towards the needs of the teacher as classroom practitioner and member of the school community. Need identification, it follows, must be a matter for negotiation between the interested parties, rather than prescription by one at the expense of the other. This suggests school and wider community environments in which relationships are collaborative rather than competitive, integrative rather than separated. It suggests leaders who are stewards of the learning of teachers. The policies of the Teacher Training Agency in relation to the extension of a national curriculum for teacher training beyond the initial phase, the prescription of national priorities for continuing professional development, and the development of standards for teachers at four stages in their careers, will undoubtedly drive a particular managerialist oriented vision of professionalism in the foreseeable future. Whether these policies will be flexible enough to be compatible with the vision of teachers as learners within a learning community put forward in this chapter is, however, a major question which Mahony and Hextall (1997) explore in their work on effective teachers for effective schools.

If the ambitions of society are to be realized, policymakers must move beyond the rhetoric in which teachers are recognized as the school's greatest asset, and beyond the exhortations for greater efforts and increased knowledge and skills – important though these are. Learning organizations will need to recognize the natural connection between a person's work life and all other aspects of life. They will need to recognize that learning is lifelong.

Personal development profiles

Throughout the business world, investment in the whole person as worker is recognized as crucial to the health of the organization. Sir Graham Day, addressing the First Rover Learning Business Open Conference, 'Learning to Win', in 1993, pointed to its importance: 'Neither the corporate learning process nor the individual one is optional. If the company seeks to survive and prosper, it must learn. If the individual, at a minimum, seeks to remain employed, let alone progress, learning is essential' (Rover 1994).

Rover recognizes that *continuous learning* is needed for those involved in change. The learning opportunities are designed not only 'to enhance job skills and acquire new technologies', but, just as important, 'to expand personal and corporate vision, thus creating the environment and opportunities for innovation. Support given to individual learning enhances ownership of and commitment to the company's goals' (Rover 1994: 3). The foundation stone of this ownership concept is the *personal development file* in which each employee ('associate')

> summarises their own learning and skills gained both through experience and formal education. It then forms a solid platform for a personal development plan, created jointly by the individual and manager, to meet the career aspirations of the individual and the business needs of the company.
>
> [Rover 1994: 7]

In an article predicted to appear in the *Education Guardian* on 14 May 2004, Michael Barber builds upon this notion, and the vision of the National Commission on Education, that every teacher should formulate and sustain a self-managed development profile. He wrote of a 1997 'Teaching Profession Act' which, 'for the first time, made teachers the subject, not the object, of reform'. He wrote:

> The best thing in the Act was the most controversial at the time. The idea that every five years in order to carry on teaching you had to present a Professional Development Profile to a mixed group of your peers from other schools and some parents of students from your own school.
>
> [Barber 1994b]

My own work with nine local education authorities and 300 teachers over three years reflects these views (Day 1995). There are six principles which underpin the notion of personal development profiling. First, teacher development is lifelong, continuing if not continuous. Secondly, it must be self-managed and, at certain times, it will involve others – teachers cannot be self-sufficient. Thirdly, it must be supported and resourced. Fourthly, it will be in the interests of the teacher and the school, though not always simultaneously. Fifthly, there must be an accounting process; and sixthly, whilst every teacher has a right and responsibility to engage in development over a career, it must be differentiated according to individual need.

Personal development profiles must be designed so that they enable the career-long development of teachers as whole persons, recognizing that 'There is a natural connection between a person's work life and all other aspects of life' (Senge 1990: 307) and, therefore, that personal mastery in all aspects of life must be supported; recognizing that teachers are not technicians, but that teaching is 'bound up with their lives, their biographies, the kind of people they have become' (Fullan, in Hargreaves 1994). It will therefore contain but not be dominated by competences. Because profiles will be lifelong, and because teacher development, like that of children, will relate to individual history as well as present circumstance, they will need to be based upon principles of differentiation, balance, and continuity and progression, and a view of learning as interdependent as well as independent. They will allow, at different times in a teaching career, for the kinds of development which might be predominantly focused upon the personal need (of the teacher as human being) and long-term professional need (of the teacher as a member of a learner community of professionals), as well as the needs of the classroom practitioner and member of a particular school. The creation of personal development planning support mechanisms over a career, which involve opportunities for both the enhancement of job skills and the development of personal and organizational vision, is not simply desirable for teachers in the twenty-first century, *it is essential*.

To develop schools we must be prepared to develop teachers. A first step in this process is to help teachers to remind themselves that they do make a difference to the lives of students. For this, a sense of vision of what might be must be ever-present.

The renewal of vision

Making a difference: developing professional judgement

A sense of vision is particularly important for teachers and schools because in the years up to and into the twenty-first century they will be expected to *make a difference* in the lives of children and young people in changing circumstances. Governments will continue to rely upon education as a means of increasing their economic competitiveness. My vision for the twenty-first century is that *good teaching* will be recognized as work which involves both the head and the heart, that it is in the first instance an interpersonal activity, 'directed at shaping and influencing (not moulding), by means of a range of pedagogical skills what people become as persons through whatever it is that is taught' (Sockett 1993: 13). It is important that teachers of the twenty-first century are able to use a range of pedagogical skills which fit their purposes. The point is that they will need not only to acquire these skills but, more importantly, to exercise pedagogical judgement – what Donald Schon calls reflection in action and van Manen, more accurately, terms *pedagogical tact* (van Manen 1995).

For the sake of quality, fundamentals of teaching and learning must be revisited. There must be a public recognition that effective learning involves, essentially, an 'interactive chemistry' between learner and teacher which depends as much on process as on content, and is an expression of personal values and perceptions as much as knowledge. Ethics and values, therefore, must play an explicit role alongside rational concerns. *The diminishing sense of agency or control that many teachers report must be replaced by a sense of accountability with trust.*

Learning partnerships: changing roles

The telecommunications revolution will inevitably enlarge the role of the individual, with more access to information and greater ability to communicate with anyone, anywhere, at any time. As a result, the boundaries between in-school and out-of-school learning will become more blurred, and teachers' roles as 'expert knowledge holders' will be eroded. Instead they will become knowledge brokers, skilled in and stewards of learning processes; for whilst technologies escalate our hopes for a better life, we regularly find ourselves unable to harness their potential! Their application in school depends upon resources way beyond those currently in place and, more importantly, upon the understanding and skills of teachers to facilitate and problematize their use. There are two issues which must be addressed alongside the growing use of the new technologies. Both suggest that the teacher's role in learning will need to be redefined.

First, much of the learning will not require the use of social skills. Yet students will continue to need to 'reflect and exchange ideas and views with other pupils and their teacher if learning is to be consolidated' (Bennett 1994). There is some evidence that even now, in primary schools, one-to-one teacher–child interactions are brief and (for most children) infrequent, and collaborative work rare (Alexander 1994). The teacher's role will therefore be as mediator rather than content expert.

Secondly, the new technologies emphasize that learning is not only the result of school experience but also of other influences – the home, the media and friends. Teachers, parents and others, then, will have an increasingly *shared responsibility* for educating children. Whilst technologies facilitate and enhance the *provision* of education, 'the educator's role is to preserve the human component *because human interaction is the key to the successful application of communication technologies to the delivery of lifelong learning*' (Stanford 1994). Schooling will perforce become more of a partnership, and 'learning contracts' between teachers, pupils and parents will become established on a more explicit basis. *Learning, if not teaching, will*

become everyone's business. Charles Handy may well be proved right in his pre-
diction that: 'instead of a *National* Curriculum for education, what is really needed
is an *individual* curriculum for every child, within common guidelines maybe, but
given expression in a formal contract between the home and the school' (Handy
1989: 21).

Whilst the National Curriculum may survive, it will be used as a means of
generating the understanding, critical thinking skills and intellectual flexibility
demanded by industry. Alongside this, the need in schools for 'moral' understanding and clarification of values will become an explicit part of every teacher's role
as he or she prepares pupils for an uncertain world in which neither the corporate
learning process nor the individual one is optional if the individual, at a minimum,
seeks to remain employed, let alone progress – a world in which lifelong learning
will be central to survival.

The teacher as pragmatic visionary

In conclusion, my vision for teachers in the next millennium is that they will be
valued, and will value themselves, both for their pragmatism and their vision, and
that their confidence and self-esteem will be enhanced by a recognition and valuing
of their essential qualities of honesty, courage, care, fairness and practical wisdom
(Sockett 1993) by politicians of every creed and the communities which they serve.
Teachers *do* trade in truth, learning *is* difficult: and providing opportunities for the
development of people is a complex process which demands infinite care and a
continuing demand for commitment, enthusiasm and integrity as well as a high
level of craft knowledge and practical wisdom.

The individualism (not individuality) of teaching will have given way, finally, to
forms of collegiality in schools among staff, which will promote rather than restrict
possibilities for good teaching.

> What sensible organisation would forbid its workers to ask their colleagues
> for help, would expect them to carry all relevant facts in their heads, would
> require them to work in 35 minute spells and then move to a different site,
> would work them in groups of 30 or over and prohibit any social interaction
> except at official break times.

[Handy 1989: 173]

The everyday conditions of schooling often mean that we spend a disproportion-
ate amount of time coping with the immediate demands of our job. Yet if we lose
sight of why we are doing it we may have an unclear view of what is really
important to us. Personal mastery involves *continual* clarification and questioning
of purpose and learning to see current reality more clearly – 'The juxtaposition of
vision (what we want) and a clear picture of current reality (where we are relative
to what we want) generates what we call "creative tension"' (Senge 1990: 142).
Vision has been a central theme of school improvement and school culture studies

worldwide over recent years (Pettigrew 1979; Bormann 1983; Wilson and Corbett 1983; Herriott and Firestone 1984; Hallinger and Murphy 1989; Louis and Miles 1990). In the twenty-first century this will be recognized as an important aspiration of teachers.

> Organizations intent on building shared visions continually encourage members to develop their personal visions. If people don't have their own vision, all they can do is 'sign up' for someone else's. The result is compliance, never commitment. On the other hand, people with a strong sense of personal direction can join together to create a powerful synergy toward what I/we truly want.
>
> [Senge 1990: 211]

Visions, then, must be created, communicated and maintained. They are socially constructed. They are not abstract. Vision is part of the daily life of the teacher. It goes beyond the maps which inform.

In the twenty-first century, as now, all good schools will be learning organizations for teachers as well as for pupils. Part of their school development plan will be a policy for continuing professional development which will enable teachers to have increased opportunities for sustained reflection through this examination of thinking and practice. It will recognize that their conditions of service (the very complexity of working in an environment which demands a large number of finely judged, differentiated interchanges and the constant exercise of reasoned judgement and intuition) have the inevitable effect of focusing their minds and hearts on short-term perspectives and increasing their dependence 'on the experiential knowledge necessary for day-to-day coping, to the exclusion of knowledge beyond their own classroom experience' (Fullan 1991: 34).

The means by which visions as well as craft may be created, developed, reviewed and renewed will be the *Personal Development Profile, a learning contract* between the teacher, the community and the school. It will guarantee for the community that the teacher will continue throughout a career to provide the knowledge, skills, commitment, care and vision appropriate to the needs of pupils; it will guarantee for the school that the teacher will fully participate in maintaining its growth as a learning organization; and it will guarantee for the teacher that both school and community will provide tangible support and genuine commitment and encouragement for his/her development.

The task of contributing to the shaping of what people become morally attracts many whose motives are idealistic (Goodlad 1990) and altruistic (Lortie 1975). Thus 'many teachers have a moral vision, a moral sense, and a moral motive however mixed up they may be in any individual person' (Sockett 1993: 14). Teaching has an essentially moral purpose in the sense that it is always concerned with the betterment or good of pupils (Noddings 1987: 23; Sockett 1989a, 1989b, 1993; Elbaz 1992). Just as the government is concerned with the betterment of schools, so headteachership is always concerned with the betterment or good of teachers.

What is deemed 'good' will of course vary across cultures and individuals. What is clear, though, is that if society demands – and it has every right to demand – teaching of the highest quality, teachers themselves must be more than pedagogical experts. Professional development opportunities in the twenty-first century must provide support for classroom pedagogy that goes far beyond the mechanics of teaching. Successful subject-specific teaching will always be sensitive to the human qualities and potential of the students. Teaching involves a moral commitment to serve the interests of students and society. It involves knowledge and expertise and accountability but it also involves *ideals*: 'Only by seeing the interplay between ideals of service, purposes and practices can the professional comprehend the moral role' (Sockett 1993).

It is the creation and sustenance of the moral and professional purposes of teachers which should provide the main agenda for their continuing professional development. It follows, therefore, that the development and maintenance of good teaching will be seen as a priority for government and for school leaders as well as for teachers themselves. All three share the responsibility to review effectiveness and work for improvement.

Those who are responsible for policy and its implementation in the twenty-first century, therefore, must acknowledge – and all who teach must assert – that experience alone will not guarantee good teaching, that not all teachers develop along a linear pathway from novice through advanced beginner to becoming competent, proficient and finally expert (Dreyfus and Dreyfus 1986). They must recognize that there are complications in sustaining the application of enthusiasm, commitment and moral purpose across a career span because of the complexities and sheer hard work of leading, day in and day out, 30 or more individuals who may or may not wish to learn, in circumstances and in environments which are not always conducive to high-quality teaching and learning. They must invest in teachers.

References

Alexander (1994) *Innocence and Experience: Reconstructing Primary Education.* Stoke on Trent: Trentham.

Barber, M. (1994a) Born to be better, *Times Educational Supplement*, 18 March, p. 19.

Barber, M. (1994b) Power and control in education 1994–2004. *British Journal of Educational Studies*, 11(4).

Beare, H. and Slaughter, R. (1993) *Education for the Twenty-First Century.* London: Routledge.

Bormann, E.G. (1983) Symbolic convergence: Organisational communication and culture, in L.L. Putman and P.E. Pacanowsley (eds) *Communication and Organisations: An Interpretive Approach.* Beverley Hills: Sage.

Buck, N., Gershuny, J., Rose, D. and Scott, J. (eds) (1994) *Changing Households: The British Household Panel Study 1990–1992.* ESRC.

Carnevale, A.P. (1994) *Quality Education: School Reform for the New American Economy.* Keynote Lecture, 1st Global Conference on Lifelong Learning, Rome.

Clarke, R. (1995) quoted in G. Haigh, To be handled with care, *Times Educational Supplement*, 19 February, p. 3.

Cockett, M. and Tripp, J. (1994) *Rowntree Trust Report*. London: Joseph Rowntree Trust.

Day, C. (1995) Professional learning and school development in action: A personal development planning project, in R. McBride (ed.) *Teacher Education Policy: Some Issues Arising from Research and Practice*. London: Falmer Press.

Dreyfus, H. and Dreyfus, S. (1986) *Mind over Machine: The Power of Human Intuition and Expertise in the Era of the Computer*. New York: The Free Press.

Elbaz, F. (1992) Hope, attentiveness and caring for difference: The moral voice. *Teaching and Teacher Education*, 8(5/6): 421–32.

ETUCE (1994) *Teacher Education*, Document 4c (point 5c). Luxembourg: Centre Jean Monnet.

Fullan, M.G. (1991) *The New Meaning of Educational Change*. New York: Teachers College Press.

Goodlad, J.I. (1990) *Teachers for Our Nation's Schools*. San Francisco: Jossey-Bass.

Hackett, C. (1995) Woodhead castigates progressives, *Times Educational Supplement*, 27 January, p. 3.

Hallinger, P. and Murphy, J. (1989) Defining an organisational mission in schools. Paper presented to AERA, Chicago, April 1992.

Handy, C. (1989) *The Age of Unreason*. London: Business Books Ltd.

Hargreaves, A. (1994) *Changing Teachers, Changing Times*. London: Cassell.

Herriott, R.E. and Firestone, W.A. (1984) Two images of schools as organisations: A refinement and elaboration. *Educational Administration Quarterly*, 20(4): 41–57.

Lortie, D.C. (1975) *Schoolteacher: A Sociological Study*. Chicago: University of Chicago Press.

Louis, S.K. and Miles, M.B. (1990) *Improving the Urban High School: What Works and Why*. New York: Teachers College Press.

Mahony, P. and Hextall, I. (1997) Effective teachers for effective schools, in R. Slee, S. Tomlinson and G. Viner (eds) *Effective for Whom*. London: Falmer Press.

McRae, H. (1995) The privilege of unemployment, *Independent on Sunday*, 26 February, p. 4.

Ministry of Education (1991) *Year 2000: A Framework for Learning: Enabling Learners*, Report of the Sullivan Commission. British Columbia, Canada.

Naisbitt, J. (1994) *Global Paradox*. New York: Avon Books.

National Commission on Education (1993) *Learning to Succeed*, Report of the Paul Hamlyn Foundation. London: Heinemann.

Noddings, N. (1987) Fidelity in teaching, teacher education, and research for teaching. *Harvard Educational Review*, 56(4): 496–510.

Pettigrew, A. (1979) On studying organisational culture. *Administrative Sciences Quarterly*, 24(4): 570–82.

Rover (1994) *Learning Business, Learning Organisation*.

Rubin (1989) The thinking teacher: Cultivating pedagogical intelligence. *Journal of Teacher Education*, 40(6): 31–4.

Senge, P. (1990) *The Fifth Discipline*. New York: Doubleday.

Sockett, H. (1989a) A moral epistemology of practice. *Cambridge Journal of Education*, 19(1): 33–41.

Sockett, H. (1989b) Research, practice and professional aspiration within teaching. *Journal of Curriculum Studies*, 21(2): 97–112.

Sockett, H. (1993) *The Moral Base for Teacher Professionalism*. New York: Teachers College Press.

Stanford, B. (1994) *Using Technology for Lifelong Learning – Strategies for Relevance in Flexible and Distance Learning*. Keynote Lecture, 1st Global Conference on Lifelong Learning, Rome.

Toombs, I. (1994) Education, culture and the arts: The relevance to industry, in A. Worsdale (ed.) *Arts, Culture and Education*. National Foundation for Arts Education, Spendlove Centre, Enstone Road, Charlbury, Oxford.

van Manen, M. (1995) On the epistemology of reflective practice. *Teachers and Teaching: Theory and Practice*, 1(1): 33–50.

Walker, J. (1995) Parenting in the 1990s. *RSA Journal*, CXLIII(5456): 29–41.

Wilson, B.L. and Corbett, H. (1983) Organisation and change: The effects of school linkages on the quantity of implementation. *Educational Administration Quarterly*, 19(4): 85–104.

5 THE IMPACT OF SELF-MANAGEMENT AND SELF-GOVERNMENT ON PROFESSIONAL CULTURES OF TEACHING: A STRATEGIC ANALYSIS FOR THE TWENTY-FIRST CENTURY

Brian J. Caldwell

Self-management and self-government are two major elements of the 1988 Education Reform Act. The processes and outcomes are more generally known as the local management of schools (LMS) and grant-maintained (GM) schools, with the latter achieved through the 'opting out' provision that enabled schools to apply to withdraw from their local education authority.

While the GM provision appears unique to this country, there is a counterpart of LMS in several nations. Indeed, if self-management is considered to be the systematic and consistent decentralization of authority to schools to make decisions on the allocation of resources within a centrally-determined framework, then self-management in one form or another would appear to be a global phenomenon, even though it is tightly constrained in many instances. It has been described as a megatrend in education (Caldwell and Spinks 1992).[1]

It is beyond the scope of this chapter to review the forces that shaped the trend, or to systematically describe and compare the various manifestations and their outcomes (see Caldwell 1994a for an account of these matters). It is acknowledged, however, that both phenomena are contentious (the contributions in Smyth 1993 are illustrative). The purpose of this chapter is to appraise the impact of self-management and self-government on professional cultures of teaching and to offer a strategic analysis for the twenty-first century. The chapter draws on the author's experience as researcher and consultant on the phenomena in several nations and on recent critiques by others. The analysis is presented in the form of nine contentions, with a concluding synthesis suggesting what the future may hold. The analysis deals mainly with self-management, given that this reform, rather than self-government, is an international phenomenon.

Contention 1: self-management is probably irreversible

Initiatives in self-management have been pursued by Governments of the left and of the right. The rhetoric changes from setting to setting, but the central thrust remains the same: centrally-determined frameworks; a leaner bureaucracy; the shift of responsibility, authority and accountability to schools; a better-informed community exercising more choice in schooling; and empowered leadership, especially for heads of schools.

Some critics (see those in Smyth 1993) have pointed to the naive faith of some nations in the market mechanism as an arbiter of quality in schooling, and have stated that curriculum and accountability frameworks have constrained decision-making at the school level. Researchers (see, for example, Malen *et al.* 1990; Fullan 1993) have pointed to the absence of evidence that self-management has led in cause-and-effect fashion to improvement in learning outcomes for students. Others have pointed to the cuts in public funding for schools that have occurred in some places at the same time that self-management has been implemented, noting that some schools have been 'winners' and others 'losers' in the resourcing of schools (see, for example, the views of heads reported in Bullock and Thomas 1994).

In general, however, self-management has been received well, despite opposition or scepticism at the outset and shortcomings in implementation along the way. Any reading of opinion in all the nations where significant change has occurred to date suggests that most schools would not wish to return to previous, more centralized arrangements.

The research from Britain of particular relevance is that on the impact of the local management of schools, commissioned by the National Association of Headteachers (NAHT). In the final report of a three-year longitudinal study of the views of headteachers, Bullock and Thomas (1994) report the generally strong acceptance of local management (LM). The responses to two survey questions are illuminating. When asked whether 'the actual experience of LM has made me more enthusiastic toward it', levels of agreement among primary heads increased from 55 per cent in 1991 to 64 per cent in 1992 to 71 per cent in 1993. Levels of agreement among secondary heads were even higher, increasing from 68 per cent in 1991 to 78 per cent in 1992 to 83 per cent in 1993. Heads were also asked to respond to the statement 'I would welcome a return to pre-LM days'. Disagreement (suggesting a favourable experience with local management) increased among both groups: with primary heads from 70 per cent in 1991 to 76 per cent in 1992 to 81 per cent in 1993; with secondary heads from 85 per cent in 1991 and 1992 to 93 per cent in 1993. These levels of acceptance among heads are consistent with those achieved in other places, notably for the pioneering approach in Edmonton, Alberta; in New Zealand; and in the most far-reaching reform in Australia, namely Victoria.

The critique based on 'winners' and 'losers' largely ignores economic and demographic realities, with the financial context for schools being set by factors other than a decision on self-management. On the positive side, the trend to self-management has been characterized by a transparency in relation to funding that has no parallel in the recent history of state education. There is now greater awareness of what resources schools receive and why, and more vigorous debate about the principles on which schools should be funded in the future.

Despite these critiques and concerns, the reality is that there has been general acceptance of self-management, and recent reports in this country point to its irreversibility. While there is some continuing uncertainty in relation to GM and private schools, the broad framework of local management is now widely accepted. The issues now are to improve approaches to governance at the local and school levels, to achieve a greater measure of equity in the allocation of resources, and to effect an increase in the overall level of resourcing of state schooling. In essence, then, a paradigm shift in the governance of public education may well be clinched by events in this country, whatever the political outcomes.

In general, taking an international perspective, self-management is long overdue; is consistent with developments elsewhere in the public and private sectors, in education and in other fields of endeavour; and is probably irreversible.

Contention 2: the significance of reform to date is not widely understood

The significance of reforms in self-management is not widely understood in two senses: first, in respect to their scope. Having studied them on four continents over 20 years, it seems to me it is only now, in the mid to late 1990s, that there is wide recognition that they are an international phenomenon. While one can still attend conferences and read publications that give little or no recognition to experience elsewhere, or that attribute developments to some grand conspiracy, there seems to be growing understanding and acceptance that public education, like virtually every other field of public and private endeavour, is engaged in long overdue restructuring.

The second, more serious sense in which the reforms have not always been well understood, is at the level of the classroom. For many teachers, they appear arbitrary and unconnected with efforts to improve the quality of learning and teaching. When combined with the effects of recession or crises in public sector finance, they have been seen as an attempt to dismantle the state system of education. Teachers, for the most part, are hard-pressed to keep abreast of developments in their field, especially in seeing 'the big picture' in school reform.

More positively, it is likely that recent developments in this country, and those foreshadowed, will clear the scene to the point where undivided attention can be given to reform at the classroom level, and this is the subject of the third contention.

Contention 3: self-management, though now broadly accepted, is by itself insufficient, providing only the preconditions for real school reform

There is an emerging view that recent reforms have not gone far enough; they may be necessary, but they are not sufficient. Critiques from three nations are very clear on this point.

In the USA, the concept of 'reinventing Government' (based on Osborne and Gaebler 1993) has shaped recent efforts to restructure the public sector, and it was only a matter of time before there was a call for 'reinventing education'. Gerstner and his colleagues (Gerstner *et al.* 1994) have presented such an argument with rare force and focus:

> The secret of American economic and political vitality is our greatest social invention: mass education, and the commitment to educate all our citizens at public expense. However, ironically, this one most vital area of our national life – public education – has not undergone the ... process of revitalising change. In our economic and social life we expect change, but in the public schools we have clung tenaciously to the ideas and techniques of earlier decades and even previous centuries.
>
> [Gerstner *et al.* 1994: 3]

> ... schools as institutions have lacked the mechanism for self-renewal. Unlike businesses that are periodically forced to respond to new technologies, new demands from their markets, or the obsolescence of their products, no external forces have demanded that schools change. Schools have been able to ignore the revolutionary possibilities of technology, to keep the same hierarchical organisational structure, to preserve traditional rules governing the numbers of students in each class and type of school, and to stick with the traditional curriculum and teaching styles used throughout this century. The schools have not gotten worse, they have simply not changed for the better.
>
> [Gerstner *et al.* 1994: 11]

Gerstner and his colleagues provide an agenda for reform which has implications for virtually every level of government and every organization with a role to play in school education.

In Britain, the effectiveness of recent major reforms has been questioned by David Hargreaves, Professor of Education at Cambridge University, in his monograph *The Mosaic of Learning: Schools and Teachers for the New Century*

(Hargreaves 1994). He considers that 'all these revolutions have largely failed' (p. 2), contending that 'Schools are still modelled on a curious mix of the factory, the asylum and the prison' (p. 43). He argues that:

> the continuing and now more urgent need to raise educational standards, in the face of increasing international competition, and to produce a nation where the average level of achievement is far higher than it is today, is becom-' ing such a powerful driver of change that many hitherto taken-for-granted assumptions about schools must now be questioned.
>
> [Hargreaves 1994: 2–3]

For Hargreaves, efforts to restructure have not gone far enough. Indeed, he contends that 'the government should go the whole hog and abolish local education authorities so that all schools become self-managing, funded from central government on the basis of a national formula' (Hargreaves 1994: 18–19). Elements of Hargreaves's reform agenda are taken up later in this paper.

In Australia, the case for refocusing the reform effort was presented in a report by Dean Ashenden, commissioned by the National Industry Education Forum (Ashenden 1994a, b):

> The present raft of reforms will make little or no headway on ... fundamental problems. National goals for schooling, the development of national curriculum profiles, decentralization of the big school systems, softening of zoning for government schools and other measures address the right problems, but cannot overcome them.
>
> The greatest single weakness in these reforms is that they stop at the classroom door. The classroom is the student's workplace. It is, in essence, a nineteenth century workplace – much more humane and interesting but recognisably the same place. It is an inefficient and inequitable producer of the old basics and simply incompatible with the new.
>
> [Ashenden 1994b: 13]

Taken together, these are formidable critiques of reforms in Australia, Britain and the USA. They support Drucker's view that 'no other institution faces challenges as radical as those that will transform the school' (Drucker 1993).

Contention 4: advances in technology will energize the next stage of school reform

The scale of the reform agenda is daunting if one appraises the readiness of schools to adopt the new learning technologies. The views of the critics are devastating. Gerstner *et al.* (1994) and Dixon (1994) start with the failure of schools to keep pace with change:

> Despite the invention of a staggering array of new information tools that store and communicate knowledge, and that entertain, challenge and extend the

power of their users, schools transmit information as they have since Gutenberg ... There is, to be sure, in some schools the promise of higher technology; a faint sense that things can and should be different. But this is the exception rather than the norm.

[Gerstner *et al.* 1994: 12]

Worldwide, school is a puffer belly locomotive chugging incongruously through a high-tech landscape.

[Dixon 1994]

Seymour Papert, inventor of Logo, comments on the actions of school administrators in limiting the exciting learning opportunities of the computer:

When there were few computers in the school, the administrator was content to leave them in the classrooms of teachers who showed greatest enthusiasm ... But as the number grew ... it made more sense to put the computers together in one room – misleadingly named 'computer lab' – under the control of a specialised computer teacher. Now all the children could come together and study computers for an hour a week. By an inexorable logic the next step was to introduce a curriculum for the computer ... Instead of cutting across and so challenging the very idea of subject boundaries, the computer now defined a new subject; instead of changing the emphasis from impersonal curriculum to excited live exploration by students, the computer was now used to reinforce the school's ways.

[Papert 1993: 39]

Some schools are now embracing the new technologies in the manner envisaged by Papert. The school as a workplace for teachers and students is indeed being reinvented. Methodist Ladies College in Melbourne is an outstanding example; most students at both primary and secondary levels now have their own lap-top computers and use them across the curriculum. Advanced interactive multimedia learning programs are now being used or trialled in many school systems. Thousands of schools around the world have access to the Internet and are interacting with schools in scores of nations. There may be an international learning network, even an international curriculum, before there is agreement on a national curriculum in some countries!

The fear that technology will replace the teacher is now exposed. Technology enriches and supports the work of teachers and students in ways previously unimagined. With an array of professional, para-professional and administrative support, teachers may be liberated from expectations that are now impossible to satisfy. The fear that technology may constrain the curriculum is also exposed. In Australia, for example, recent policy statements by Government and opposition at the national level explicitly linked the new technologies with a celebration of the cultural life of the nation.

There is, of course, the issue of equity. It is palpably clear that there are disparities among schools and students in access to learning technology. This should not be construed as an argument against setting a high priority on this item in the new agenda for reform. It simply raises the stakes in resourcing the transformation.

Contention 5: a new organizational image is required for schools

These stakes are even higher when one contemplates the fabric of schools. Most schools do not provide an environment conducive to learning. Indeed, many are among the shabbiest structures to be found in their communities. They should be pulled down and replaced by attractive workplaces for learning in the twenty-first century.

David Hargreaves (1994: 54) called for schools to be better equipped with the new interactive technologies in his vision of schools for the twenty-first century, but argued that schools as currently constructed are obsolete:

> Schools must be constructed on the basis of a new institutional model before the technologies will be admitted and allowed to develop to their full potential. Factories are disappearing; modern businesses look very unlike the nineteenth century heavy-industry factory . . . We are glad to see the end of the traditional factory; why should we expect the school modelled on it to be welcome to children.
>
> [Hargreaves 1994: 43–4]

Hargreaves proposed a shift in image, from the factory to the hospital. From the nineteenth century, we constructed our schools to resemble factories of that era, with students progressing from grade to grade, from room to room, as in a production line. Principles of school management were based on those in industry. Our schools have changed little: classrooms for students, teachers with limited administrative support, a small number of para-professionals and, with few exceptions, only modest advances in technology. Compare this with the modern hospital, with its astonishing array of technology, individual rooms, elective surgery, and complex professional and para-professional staffing structure.

The opening lines of Seymour Papert's *The Children's Machine* invite the same shift in thinking. He asks the reader to imagine time travellers from an earlier century, including a group of surgeons and a group of teachers, eager to see what changes have occurred in their professions over the last century. For the visitor to the hospital, 'they would in almost all cases be unable to figure out what the surgeon was trying to accomplish or what was the purpose of the many strange devices . . . the surgical staff were employing'; for the visitor to the school, 'they would fully see the point of most of what was being attempted and could quite easily take over the class'. Papert concludes that 'In the wake of the startling growth of science and technology in our recent past, some areas of human activity have undergone megachange . . . School is a notable example of an area that has not' (Papert 1993: 1–2).

Not all will warm to Hargreaves's image of the school as hospital. It may be better than school as factory, but it is not right. Some have called for schools to be high-reliability or 'no defects' organizations, much like the airline industry, where failures are taken very seriously. The crash of a plane results in protracted and expensive inquiries; we are only now starting to take seriously the 'crash' of a school.

Clearly, of course, we need a new image of *school as school*, but it is crucial that we reject the factory image and, even playfully, try others.

Contention 6: there will be major change to teaching as a 'job'

If we were to 'start again' with our design of schools as buildings and as places of work for students and teachers, they would look very different from those we lead and manage today. It is beyond the scope of this chapter to provide the specifications, but Gerstner *et al.*'s (1994) concept of 're-inventing education' or a derivative of Hammer and Champy's (1994) concept of 're-engineering' may well apply.

Further change energized by advances in technology, a new organizational image, and facilities that are more welcoming to students and teachers will be major elements in a re-engineered school. Another element is likely to be the 'job' of teaching. Hargreaves calls for changes in schools for the twenty-first century which should:

▶ have a core of full-time, highly trained professional teachers, on five-year renewable contacts, supported by a range of assistant teachers and part-time teachers who also work in other fields;
▶ contract out substantial parts of their teaching functions, so that secondary pupils spend less of their time in school;
▶ be permeable to their community, to business and the world of working adults, so that the boundaries between school and the outside world weaken (Hargreaves 1994: 53–4).

More fundamental, however, is the manner in which all work and the concept of a 'job' is changing. These changes are described by William Bridges in his recent book *Jobshift* (Bridges 1995). He argues that '*the job* is not going to be part of tomorrow's economic reality'. He is referring here to the concept of a person working full-time and long-term for a particular organization. Arguing from a view that 'the job is a social artifact', he contends that:

> The job concept emerged in the eighteenth and nineteenth centuries to package the work that needed doing in the growing factories and bureaucracies of the industrialising nations. Before people had jobs, they worked just as hard but on shifting clusters of tasks, in a variety of locations, on a schedule set by the sun, the weather and the needs of the day. The modern job was a

startling new idea ... Now the world of work is changing again. The very conditions (mass production and the large organisation) that created jobs two hundred years ago are disappearing.

[Bridges 1995: viii–ix]

Bridges writes almost exclusively about jobs in business, but the very forces he identifies as shaping change in that field are impacting on education, and the chief among these is technology. The kinds of change he describes for business, which are advocated to some extent by Hargreaves for schools, are already evident in education. Why should we expect that education will or should be buffered against such change, particularly when it may be the means by which a range of specialist professional and para-professional support can enhance the processes of learning and teaching?

Bridges suggests that yesterday's organization located every person vertically in a hierarchy and horizontally in a functional unit, with a formal job description and a career path up the hierarchy with corresponding increases in power and reward (Bridges 1995: 50–1). He extends Charles Handy's view of tomorrow's organization as a three-leaf shamrock. For Handy, one leaf is the core of professional, technical, managerial staff; another is made up of external contractors who provide specialist support; the third consists of 'contingent' workers, who are temporary or part-time people who come and go as needed. Bridges suggests that these leaves are more permeable or transient than presented by Handy (Bridges 1995: 156–8).

These developments are of course already evident in education, but we have tended to view them as more dysfunctional and an aberration than as extensive, fundamental and inevitable change in the sense described by Bridges. Nonetheless, many professionals in education are already accommodating this new (old) concept of 'job' and are finding themselves a rewarding and satisfying niche in a reshaped profession.

Contention 7: new reward schemes will be required for those who work in schools

An immediate implication is the need to restructure the traditional reward scheme for those who work in schools. Certainly, a scheme that reflects the hierarchical organizational model must be changed to reflect flatter structures and weaker bureaucracies. The smaller full-time 'continuing' professional core may remain salaried, but at much higher levels, given its level of responsibility for school success. Fee-for-service arrangements are more likely to suit school needs as well as individual needs for others in Bridges's expanded view of the Handy shamrock. For the longer term, Bridges suggests that:

Whether by means of pay for skills, fee for service, share of the earnings, or some still-to-be-discovered form of compensation, the organization of the future is going to find that salaries are as counterproductive as jobs. It is a truism that you get what you pay for, and with organizations needing to get new levels of effort and new degrees of flexibility from their workers, new kinds of compensation are going to be commonplace.

[Bridges 1995: 166]

Another view of the importance of rewards may be derived from Lawler's prescription for high performance in decentralized organizations (Lawler 1986, 1992). He proposes four dimensions: structures and powers; knowledge and skill; information; and rewards. It is apparent that matters related to structures and powers have already been addressed, but the others are not well-developed. Knowledge and skill are addressed later in this chapter; the focus here is on rewards. Essentially, Lawler challenges us to devise a system of rewards that is consistent with the new structures and that focuses on performance. Expressed another way, governments have been preoccupied with changes in structure and power, but high performance in the self-managing school will not be achieved without new systems of rewards for those who work in schools, in addition to new levels of knowledge and skill.

Career structures that reflect levels of professional competence should replace those based exclusively on positions in an organizational hierarchy. A focus on performance does not imply yesterday's discredited merit-pay schemes, but a form of 'gain-sharing' that rewards the contribution an employee makes to school success, whether that be for a particular school improvement project or sustained long-term gains in a single subject or across the curriculum. Moreover, such a scheme is more likely than in the past to reward the efforts of a team, for our experience in education and in other fields points to the importance of the team in the achievement of high performance. It is noteworthy that the new career structure for teachers in state schools in Victoria, Australia, encourages rewards for members of high-performing teams, in addition to providing higher levels of reward for leading that do not relate to levels of an organizational hierarchy (see Odden and Odden 1994 for research on school self-management in Victoria using a framework derived from Lawler's four dimensions).

Contention 8: there may be a case for reinventing preparation and professional development programmes for teachers, with universities playing a key role

Lawler's prescription for high performance in a decentralized organization included knowledge and skills. In the school setting this is a call for all who work in schools, or who serve schools, to have the knowledge and skills to work in a self-managing school where further reform of the kind described is likely to occur. While governments have addressed to some extent the needs of heads and governors, it is clear that the needs of teachers should move, belatedly, to centre stage.

Education of the profession is perhaps the highest priority in the further transformation of school education. A shift away from the factory image towards the hospital image suggests a rich array of professionals at the school level. The role of teacher should change along the lines advocated by Gerstner and his colleagues in their case for reinventing education in the USA. Teachers should be coaches, counsellors, learning managers, participants, leaders, learners, authors and futurists.

There are implications for a range of institutions. The previous Government in Britain had a preference for placing funds for teacher training in the hands of schools, which would then buy services from universities or other providers. This was clearly an effort to 'reinvent' or 're-engineer' teacher education. However, while closer links with schools and other work settings are important, the scope and complexity of change as described in this chapter suggest a major role for the faculty of education. While vigorous scholarly debate and a comprehensive research agenda will be critically important, academics generally will need to work within the new organizational paradigm of self-management which is now settling into place.

Expectations for school education also suggest a demanding agenda for the professional development of teachers. Full resourcing from the public sector, while desirable, is unlikely to be achieved. A more likely and arguably desirable strategy is an employer contribution to what will be largely a private effort. In other words, teachers and other professionals will proceed on the same basis as their counterparts in most fields within a framework of professional expectations and standards. Fee-paying programmes of universities and other providers may be the model for future professional development in school education.

Bridges describes facets of training programmes for a future where jobs will be different from now. For example, he contends that 'management training is going to have to become training in coaching and consulting rather than training in oversight and control'; that 'the future employee-development programme is going to be much more like a programme for self-employed entrepreneurs than a programme for job holders'; and that 'self-directed education is . . . going to have to be supplemented with organizationally sponsored business-development opportunities, so that someone who sees an unmet need or a problem that needs solving can get funding to tackle it' (Bridges 1995: 170). While it is acknowledged that he is writing mainly for the non-education sector, the main themes here are likely to be evident in the professional development of teachers.

In general, this contention and its associated strategies are a call for the re-skilling of the profession. To sustain an outdated organizational image for school, or to expect that the job of teaching will not change as the rest of the world of work changes, will have the effect of de-skilling the profession.

Contention 9: there should be a shift in the concept of self-management, from the institution to the individual

Implied in the foregoing is recapturing the original concept of self-management, for it referred to the self-management of one's own work and development. However, Bridges proposed a shift in this concept:

The old concept was 'taking care of yourself' while you followed the leader. The new self-management is 'acting toward the business at hand (learning and the support of learning in the case of the school) as if you had an ownership stake in it'.

[Bridges 1995: 167]

This does not mean, however, that teachers will return to what many perceive as a golden age of autonomy. Autonomy in state education will be constrained by curriculum and standards frameworks. These too have gained wide acceptance among those with a stake in public education: governments, the business sector, parents, students and, increasingly, teachers, despite gross flaws in design and implementation that have had to be rectified.

What will be the scope for the exercise of professional judgement by the self-managing teacher? It will be unlimited if we take seriously the mission to provide the very best of learning opportunities for every student. Leading a team of professional and para-professionals using state-of-the-art learning technologies and knowledge about learning will call for a level of professional skill that can be compared with that of a skilled surgeon. The skilled professional in medicine is constrained by protocols and must work to standards that are as demanding as will ever be faced by teachers.

Some early evidence from the Schools of the Future reform in Victoria, Australia, suggests that teachers' knowledge about learning and teaching has been enhanced through school self-management. In this reform, about 1700 schools have control over their budgets and staffing, with each having a charter that reflects an understanding between the school and its community on the one hand, and the school and the Directorate of School Education on the other, in which the school sets out the manner in which it will address the learning needs of its students within a curriculum and standards framework. Three years after implementation commenced, 85 per cent of school principals reported moderate to high improvement in learning outcomes for students (Cooperative Research Project, 1997).

There is clearly a need for further research on these developments in Victoria and elsewhere, but the point is that work in school and personal self-management, constrained by curriculum and standards frameworks as demanding as those that face the skilled professional in the medical field, provide unlimited scope for the exercise of professional judgement and the achievement of high standards of professional practice.

Strategic analysis: a synthesis of themes

This analysis suggests that the self-managing school – the locally managed school in Britain – is likely to be a feature of state education in the twenty-first century, at least in the early years of the new millennium; so too are curriculum and standards frameworks, despite flaws in design and implementation. An era of stability in these structural reforms is likely. The future of intermediate levels of governance and the self-governing school – local education authorities and grant-maintained schools in Britain – is less certain and more problematic.

While settlement on the concept of the self-managing school may be imminent, it is clear that it does not go far enough as a reform if the intention is to achieve long-term gains in the quality of schooling. Further reform must focus on learning: especially the technologies of learning, and on school as a place of work for students and teachers. The concept of teaching as *the job* is likely to change, as it will in every field of public and private endeavour, so that a range of professional and para-professional staff will serve the school, some in a more or less permanent core, and an increasing number in contractual, temporary or part-time arrangements. New reward schemes will be required, for traditional career paths and rewards based on advancement in a hierarchy will disappear. Reward in such schemes will be based on performance, including the performance of teams.

The concept of self-management will shift (return) to a focus on the individual, with plans for individual development changing in scope and focus to accommodate the shift in the concept of 'job'. While a capacity for personal self-management and the exercise of professional judgement may appear at first sight to be constrained by curriculum and standards frameworks, a comparison with the work of the skilled professional in the medical field suggests unlimited scope in achieving the mission to provide quality learning for all students. Even the most advanced professionals must work within the protocols and to the standards that are the hallmarks of their fields.

This is not a return to what some may remember as a golden era of autonomy in teaching, but it is the opportunity to work in the new paradigm of the self-managing school to advance teaching as a field of professional practice.

Note

1 The ten megatrends identified in *Leading the Self-Managing School* (Caldwell and Spinks 1992) were:

   1 There will be a powerful but sharply focused role for central authorities, especially in respect to formulating goals, setting priorities and building frameworks for accountability.
   2 National and global considerations will become increasingly important, especially in respect to curriculum and an education system that is responsive to national needs within a global economy.
   3 Within centrally determined frameworks, government (public) schools will become largely self-managing, and distinctions between government and non-government [private] schools will narrow.
   4 There will be unparalleled concern for the provision of a quality education for each individual.

5 There will be dispersion of the educative function, with telecommunications and computer technology ensuring that much learning that currently occurs in schools or in institutions of higher education will occur at home and in the workplace.
6 The basics of education will be expanded to include problem-solving, creativity and a capacity for lifelong learning and relearning.
7 There will be an expanded role for the arts and spirituality, defined broadly in each instance; there will be a high level of 'connectedness' in the curriculum.
8 Women will claim their place among the ranks of leaders in education, including those at the most senior levels.
9 The parent and community role in education will be claimed or reclaimed.
10 There will be unparalleled concern for service by those who are required or have the opportunity to support the work of schools.

References

Ashenden, D. (1994a) *Australian Schooling: Two Futures*. Paper commissioned by the National Industry Education Forum, Australia.

Ashenden, D. (1994b) Better schools begin with better classroom reform, *The Australian*, 19 October, p. 13.

Bridges, W. (1995) *Jobshift*. London: Nicholas Brealey.

Bullock, A. and Thomas, H. (1994) *The Impact of Local Management on Schools: Final Report*. Birmingham: University of Birmingham.

Caldwell, B.J. (1994) School-based management, in T. Husen and N. Postlethwaite (eds) *International Encyclopedia of Education*. London: Pergamon Press.

Caldwell, B.J. and Spinks, J.M. (1992) *Leading the Self-Managing School*. London: Falmer Press.

Cooperative Research Project (1997) *More Work to be Done But . . . No Turning Back*. Report of the Cooperative Research Project on 'Leading Victoria's Schools of the Future', Directorate of School Education, Victorian Association of State Secondary Principals, Victorian Primary Principals Association, The University of Melbourne (Fay Thomas, Chair) (available from Department of Education Policy and Management, The University of Melbourne).

Dixon, R.G.D. (1994) Future schools: How to get there from here. *Phi Delta Kappan*, 75(5): 360–5.

Drucker, P.F. (1993) *Post-Capitalist Society*. New York: HarperBusiness.

Fullan, M.G. (1993) Coordinating school and district development in restructuring, in J. Murphy and P. Hallinger (eds) *Restructuring Schooling: Learning from Ongoing Efforts*. Newberry Park, CA: Corwin Press.

Gerstner, L.V., Semerad, R.D., Doyle, D.P. and Johnston, W.B. (1994) *Reinventing Education: America's Public Schools*. New York: Dutton.

Hammer, M. and Champy, J. (1993) *Reengineering the Corporation: A Manifesto for Business Revolution*. London: Nicholas Brealey.

Hargreaves, D. (1994) *The Mosaic of Learning: Schools and Teachers for the New Century*. London: Demos.

Lawler, E.E. (1986) *High Involvement Management*. San Francisco: Jossey-Bass.

Lawler, E.E. (1992) *The Ultimate Advantage*. San Francisco: Jossey-Bass.

Malen, B., Ogawa, R. and Kranz, J. (1990) What do we know about school-based manage-
    ment? A case study of the literature – A call for research, in W.H. Clune and J.F.
    White (eds) *Choice and Control in American Schools*. Philadelphia: Falmer Press.
Odden, A. and Odden, E. (1994) 'Applying the high involvement framework to local man-
    agement of schools in Victoria, Australia', presented in a symposium on 'Improving
    School Performance Through School Based Management: A Systemic Approach' at
    the Annual Meeting of the American Educational Research Association, New Orleans,
    4 April.
Osborne, D. and Gaebler, T. (1993) *Reinventing Government*. London: Macmillan.
Papert, S. (1993) *The Children's Machine: Rethinking School in the Age of the Computer*.
    New York: BasicBooks.
Smyth, J. (ed.) (1993) *A Socially-Critical View of the Self-Managing School*. Washington,
    D.C. and London: Falmer Press.

6 REBUILDING TEACHER PROFESSIONALISM IN THE UNITED STATES

Milbrey W. McLaughlin

Calls for change in teaching and learning

America's schools and teachers confront unprecedented demands for reform. Calls to do better, and to do differently, issue from disparate sources and describe new focus and frames for teaching and learning. In a nation fond of reforming, the end of the twentieth century witnesses the most comprehensive reform agenda ever undertaken.

Challenges to traditional practices issue primarily from three sources: the standards-based reform movement; new theories of learning; the changed character and needs of America's students. These presses for change direct attention to teachers' knowledge base, ability to meet students' educational needs, and their conceptions of practice. Together, they demand rebuilding of teacher professionalism in the United States.[1]

Standards-based reform

A steady stream of reports, commissions and panels declare that what most American students know and can do is not good enough. The 1983 report, *A Nation at Risk*, cautioned the country that 'the educational foundations of society are presently being eroded by rising tides of mediocrity'. As a nation, the report warned, we were committing an 'act of unthinking, unilateral educational disarmament' (National Commission on Excellence in Education 1983).

In 1990, *America's Choice*, the report of the Commission on the Skills of the American Workforce, portrayed the US as poised on an 'economic cliff'. America, according to this assessment, was not producing a highly educated, skilful workforce, because it lacked 'a clear standard of achievement and few students are motivated to work hard in school'. The report recommended that 'new educational performance standards should be set for all students . . . and benchmarked to the highest in the world' (Commission on the Skills of the American Workforce 1990: 3–5).

The perceived mismatch between what society expects and what students can do unleashed an avalanche of initiatives to raise standards, change curriculum, tighten educators' accountability and restructure the way schools do business. These national interests were enacted at the federal level in GOALS 2000, reform legislation which relies on new content and performance standards to bring about change in classroom practices. According to the US Education Department, the strategy for GOALS 2000 is 'based on a simple idea: when more is expected of students, they work harder and reach higher levels of achievement'. GOALS 2000: Educate America Act established a framework to identify 'world class' academic standards, to measure students' progress and provide opportunities to learn. The companion School-to-Work Opportunities Act of 1994 states that participating students are expected to follow a programme of study that meets rigorous state academic content standards.

The push for standards-based reforms has been advanced by the profession. Many professional organizations have provided leadership in the development of voluntary standards for academic content and student performance. The National Council on Teachers of Mathematics (NCTM), for example, put forward a new view of mathematics and a new view of learning mathematics that embodies a shift towards logic and mathematical evidence as verification, and away from mere memorization of procedures; a shift towards conjecturing, inventing, problem-solving, and away from simply finding the right answer (National Council on Teachers of Mathematics 1991).

Other professional organizations, such as the National Center for History in the Schools, and the National Council of Teachers of English (NCTE), have followed suit in developing standards to reform teaching and learning in American classrooms. Geographers, art educators, and other subject-matter specialists likewise wrestle with the complex, difficult task of defining content standards for their practice.[2]

Taken singly or together, these standards-setting efforts portray fundamentally different ideas of what teachers should teach and students should know and be able to do. This vision of classroom teaching and learning imagines practices which are much more rigorous and demanding than those found in most American classrooms today. Further, it embraces higher expectations and standards for *all* students, not just the college-bound, on the assumption that all students can learn given adequate opportunities.

New theories of learning

Efforts to raise standards for what is learned take place in the context of a 'revolution' in cognitive science (Gardner 1985; Damasio 1994). Contrary to the teacher-dominated, transmission-oriented practices that have characterized American education, current theory holds that students learn best when they have the opportunity to actively construct their own knowledge. New theories of learning frame new conceptions about important outcomes of learning and, by extension, of school: higher-order thinking skills and deep understanding of the conceptual structures of knowledge domains. A central aim of education, in this view, is to produce young people who know how to learn (Bruer 1993).

The classroom practices that reformers envision, often described as 'teaching and learning for understanding', assume fundamental change in teachers' beliefs about content, pedagogy and students (Prawat 1992; McLaughlin and Oberman, 1996). They imply a classroom more responsive to diverse student abilities and interests, which emphasizes cooperative learning strategies, direct opportunities to construct knowledge and understanding, and performance assessments that tap students' conceptual development rather than mastery of rote knowledge.

In this reform era, American teachers are asked not only to provide more challenging teaching and learning, but to change their conceptions of the nature of teaching and learning in the classroom. Reformers are asking for a *kind of education* they have never before sought.

Today's students

Real-life classroom contexts complicate this ambitious agenda. The values, cultures, expectations and life conditions that today's students bring to school differ in fundamental ways from those of yesterday's students.

The social setting for teaching in the USA has never been more demanding. Schooling for all, perhaps America's most important social policy, has nearly been achieved.[3] However, the success of this social policy, together with the arrival of numbers of new immigrants exceeding any since the beginning of the century, has created diversity among American students far exceeding any imagined by early proponents of universal education. These have changed student demographics, particularly in California and other 'border' states, filling classrooms with students whose English skills are limited, and who may have only marginal literacy in their first language.

Further, more students stay in school longer, and more students with special needs are educated in 'mainstream' classrooms. Today's students generally have fewer family resources available to them. One out of four American children now lives in poverty; children who endure a multitude of stresses in their lives are present in virtually all classrooms. Violence in school ranks as the number one education concern among the American public.

America's reform agenda assumes a challenging curriculum and 'world class' academic standards for *all* students. The need to offer learning opportunities compatible with the needs of America's diverse student population defies a formulaic approach to 'delivery of educational services', or traditional ideas about professional development and the organization of educational environments. On these grounds alone, the challenge to American teachers is breathtaking.

challenges to teachers' professionalism

This ambitious reform agenda and the vision of teaching and learning it advances will succeed, if at all, in classroom teachers' everyday work. It presents a fundamental challenge to teachers' professionalism.

Primary among conditions that distinguish a 'profession' from other occupations are a specialized knowledge base and shared standards of practice – *technical culture*; commitment to meeting client needs – *service ethic*; strong identity with the profession – *professional commitment*; and collegiate, as opposed to bureaucratic, control over practice and the profession – *professional autonomy* (Etzioni 1969; Larson 1977; see Talbert and McLaughlin 1994 for elaboration). The vision of practice underlying the nation's reform agenda touches all elements of professionalism.

Teachers' professionalism must be rebuilt around that challenge to practice, yet there is little precedent in policy or practice to guide the effort. Teachers' work, as presently organized, provides little opportunity or incentive to tackle the difficult task that reformers outline.

Professional development in the reform era

Key to rebuilding professionalism is teachers' success in accomplishing the serious and difficult tasks of *learning* the skills and perspectives assumed by reformers and, often, *unlearning* practices and beliefs about students or instruction that have dominated their entire professional lives (Prawat 1992).

Because teaching for understanding relies on teachers' abilities to see complex subject matter from the perspectives of diverse students, the know-how necessary to accomplish this vision of practice cannot be prepackaged or conveyed by means of traditional 'teacher training' strategies. Rebuilding professionalism requires professional development opportunities that extend beyond mere support for teachers' acquisition of new skills or knowledge to comprise occasions for teachers to reflect critically on their practice and fashion new knowledge and beliefs about content, pedagogy and learners (McLaughlin and Oberman, 1996).

Professional development of this stripe signals a departure from old norms and models of 'pre-service training' or 'in-servicing' to new images of what, when and how teachers learn. These new images bring a corresponding shift from policies which seek to control or direct the work of teachers to strategies intended to *develop the capacity* of schools and teachers to be responsible for student learning. Capacity-building policies view knowledge as constructed by and with practitioners for use in their own contexts, rather than as something conveyed by policymakers as a single solution for top-down implementation.

Policy support for teachers' professional development

The need for more and different professional development opportunities for teachers is recognized at all levels of Government. At the federal level, GOALS 2000 and the reauthorized Elementary and Secondary Education Act (ESEA) pay particular attention to professional development and underscore the key role of teachers in carrying out the reform agenda.

GOALS 2000: Educate America Act establishes a framework for 'state and local education systemic improvement' that highlights professional development.[4] ESEA was constructed to complement and extend GOALS 2000 by encouraging support for professional development focused on new national standards and on teachers' capacity to work with students with limited English proficiency or with disabilities. ESEA, the largest single federal investment in K-12 education, was seen as the 'engine' whose dollars could power the ambitious but underfunded GOALS 2000.

These federal policies depart significantly from past federal efforts in that they endeavour to enable state and local professional development activities, not to specify them. These federal policies tie professional development to specific content and performance standards, represent it as ongoing, spanning teachers' careers, and integral to the daily life of schools.

At the state level, a number of initiatives are under way to provide technical assistance and other support to schools endeavouring to restructure the habits and culture of the school to enhance learning for both students and teachers. For example, California initiated a special structure, the Center for School Restructuring (CCSR), to provide technical assistance and support, based on the belief that support strategies must be co-created with participating schools and districts. CCSR's work and strategies rely on creating learning opportunities – for schools, districts, stakeholders, diverse regional support providers, and for itself – that respond to the challenges faced by restructuring schools and districts. The Center's mission is to create the climate, incentive and impetus to act on that learning (California Center for School Restructuring 1992).

These and similar state and national efforts self-consciously attempt to provide 'top-down' support for 'bottom-up' change by furnishing broad direction and resources to teachers' efforts to reinvent practice. As such, they endeavour to enhance teachers' professionalism, rather than diminish it, by increasing professional decision-making about standards of practice.

An emerging paradigm for professional development

Though the outlines of a new policy paradigm for professional development are appearing (Cohen *et al.* 1993; Darling-Hammond 1993), the hard work of developing concrete exemplars of policies and intersecting practices that model 'top-down support for bottom-up reform' has just begun. In this reform era, old models of 'staff development', 'in-servicing' or 'teacher training' are well and truly understood as inadequate and wrongheaded (Little 1993).

Ideas about *where* teachers' learning and growth take place most effectively have evolved from the hierarchical, laboratory-based models of the late 1960s, which assumed that practitioners could simply transfer knowledge from workshop to classroom (see, for example, Gagne 1968), to approaches that recognize the importance of embedding teachers' learning in everyday activities (e.g. Case and Bereiter 1984; Tharp and Gallimore 1988; Lieberman and Miller 1991). An emerging body of cognitive and social science research offers robust evidence that context and cognition are inextricably linked for all learners, be they children or adults (e.g. Lave and Wenger 1991; Rogoff 1993).

Reformers' visions also frame new ideas about *what* teachers need to learn. Teachers' learning is no longer viewed as comprising primarily accumulating fact-based knowledge, but as comprehending new conceptions of content and pedagogy, and taking on the new roles assumed by teaching and learning for understanding.

If professional development is not a 'programme' offered after school or on weekends, an event composed primarily of 'how-tos' and 'shoulds' conveyed by experts, what is it? What kinds of professional development can enable the difficult changes expected of teachers and students?

Like students, teachers learn by doing, reading and reflecting, collaborating with other teachers, looking closely at students and their work, and sharing what they see. This kind of learning enables teachers to make the leap from theory to accomplished practice. It requires settings that support teacher inquiry and collaboration, strategies grounded in teachers' questions and concerns, and a theoretically powerful base of knowledge. To understand deeply, teachers must learn about, see and experience successful learning-centred and learner-centred teaching practices.

Sustained change in teachers' learning opportunities and practices will require investments in the infrastructure of reform – development of the institutions and environmental support that will promote the spread of ideas and shared learning about how change can be attempted and sustained. Rebuilding teachers' professionalism also requires seeing 'old' activities in new ways, focusing on opportunities for engagement, learning and growth. A number of strategies emerge in the US context as especially powerful tools for rethinking teachers' professional development and enabling teachers to engage in the difficult task of rebuilding professional practice.

Rebuilding teachers' professionalism: new wine in new bottles

Efforts to rethink professional development must break new ground; autopsies of failed strategies fill the literature, but the empirical base to inform new policies and practices is limited. While a 'model' that could inform new approaches to professionalism is yet to be fleshed out, a number of promising methods suggest broad direction and opportunities for developing policies and practices.

New professional roles for teachers

The standards-based reforms in the United States have generated new roles for teachers as developers of new assessment practices and content standards. Whereas in earlier eras, reformers generally delivered curriculum packages for teachers to implement, and designated assessment systems to measure student outcomes, teachers have now become central players in designing assessments and content standards. These new professional roles for teachers have been central to rebuilding teacher professionalism in the USA.

Assessment

Reformers of all stripes agree that teacher involvement in developing assessments and in assessing student work comprises perhaps the single most potent opportunity for teachers' learning and change. Engaging teachers in conversation about what students should know and be able to do, and how that performance could be assessed, prompts teachers to look critically at their own work and question the relationship between teaching practices and student learning.

Teacher involvement in assessment activities exists from the bottom to the top of the education system. At the local level, teachers have initiated grass-roots projects to develop performance-based strategies such as portfolios which could assess the full range of what is considered important for students to know and be able to do. Within the schools, teachers use self-assessment and collective evaluation of student work as occasions to make demands on the fit between educational mission and student outcomes. Some of these school-based efforts are initiated by teachers within the school on their own. Others are stimulated by state policies and provide important opportunities for teachers to develop the capacity to use assessment to improve instruction. For example, in 1991 the California Department of Education established the California Assessment Collaborative, which supported and studied a variety of school and district-based efforts at development and implementation of alternative assessment.

The effective assessment projects supported by this state initiative are collaborative efforts in which teacher participants draft tasks or make collective decisions about the contents of a portfolio, try them out with students, and make numerous revisions based on the data from student responses. The recursive nature of the inquiry process immersed teachers in serious and often heated discussion about practice: 'The writers have revised and revised, rubrics have been made and revised and revised, and scorers have scored and argued and scored again' (Jamentz, 1996). This grass-roots assessment work becomes an action research project and powerful occasion for learning (Cochran-Smith and Lytle 1993).

Assessment initiatives at state and national levels have generated similarly powerful conversations about practice. Several states, and the national-level New Standards Project, have announced initiatives to use performance tasks in large-scale assessments that tap students' higher-order thinking skills. These efforts have worked closely with teachers to develop performance assessments. From teachers' reports, this involvement has comprised the most powerful professional development occasion of their careers.

Defining content standards

Teachers coming together around issues of content provide occasion for the kind of fundamental reconsideration of practice associated with assessment. Data collected by the Center for Research on the Contexts of Teaching at Stanford University dramatically illustrate how standards can stimulate teachers' examination of practice and change (McLaughlin and Talbert 1993). During the period of our field research, California mathematics frameworks, aligned with those developed by the NCTM, were being promoted aggressively at state and local levels. California mathematics teachers working in strong communities of practice which engaged these content concerns, reported much higher levels of successful adaptation to today's students and change in classroom practices, than did Michigan teachers. Lacking the strong push for changed content and pedagogy generated by the California reform effort, Michigan teachers working in strong professional communities instead collaborated to reinforce traditional norms of practice, strategies clearly ineffective with their non-traditional students. The California mathematics framework provided strong direction for change, and focus for teachers' reflection and construction of new classroom practices.

The US experience offers an important caveat, however, about the role of standards-based reform in rebuilding teacher professionalism. Standards such as those set out in the California framework, which provide broad direction to curriculum content but leave specification to districts and teachers, have engaged teachers in authentic conversation and debate that goes to the heart of professionalism. The extent to which new standards can serve this function depends on the specificity with which they are defined, and their inclusiveness or scope. Not all content standards developed in the USA have supported teachers' efforts to reinvent practice. The new geography standards, for example, set out more than 100 highly specific content standards. Conformity with these standards would squeeze out local discretion because few choices are left to be made, and preclude teaching much else in the secondary school curriculum if an earnest effort were made to address this lengthy list of content knowledge and competences.

Teacher learning communities: occasions for professional discourse

Traditional teacher 'training' activities that failed to provide occasion for teachers' growth and learning shared a number of features. In general, they targeted individual teachers, and involved them in centrally defined, transmission-style activities uncharacteristic of their own schools and classrooms. They were generic, decontextualized activities that offered teachers little experience with the kinds of active learning assumed by current reforms. Teachers' learning communities, operating at various levels and locations, comprise necessary and powerful occasions for teachers to learn new practices, and to unlearn old assumptions, beliefs and practices. (Indeed, many teachers comment that while it may be possible to learn alone, unlearning demands a supportive group setting.)

What is a teacher learning community? Research at the Center for Research on the Contexts of Teaching identifies many forms and constructions of a positive learning community (Talbert and McLaughlin 1994). At a minimum, the requisite seems to be at least another colleague committed to change, eager to learn, and an opportunity for discourse.

Teachers' learning communities inside school
When considered and organized as a learning community, schools and departments provide up-close occasions for professional development and rethinking norms of practice. Considering the taken-for-granted aspects of school sparks change and provides occasion for professional growth and learning.

▶ *Academic departments* self-consciously organized around learning, reflection, and collective development of practice come to resemble 'knowledge collectives', where responsibility for students' and colleagues' learning is shared. Such departments find time to meet together regularly, establish a norm of trust and problem-solving, and reframe professionalism in terms of teachers' ongoing learning and reflection (Little and McLaughlin 1994; Siskin 1994; Talbert and McLaughlin 1994; Grossman, 1996).

Departments of this sort contrast with typical department communities in US secondary schools where isolation is the rule and department meetings, when they occur, focus only on 'administrative' and bureaucratic procedures. 'We usually meet once a month,' a Michigan social studies teacher told us. 'But often the meetings get cancelled, since there is nothing to talk about.' 'Sure we meet,' joked a California biology teacher about her department gatherings. 'We meet at the mailbox on our way out of the building.' It all depends on perspective. Is the department meeting seen as an occasion for professional growth or as a tiresome obligation?

▶ *Interdisciplinary teams* of teachers cut across these organizational boundaries, making problematic traditional-subject-matter boundaries. Teacher teams wrestle with conceptions of subject matter and discipline-based ideas about student learning in ways that push participants to take a critical look at their practice and the assumptions underlying them. The Coalition of Essential Schools, for example, brings together teachers from social studies and language arts to work on a course in journalism; science and mathematics teachers collaborate on new courses focused on methods of inquiry and scientific learning. Interdisciplinary work such as this requires teachers to think deeply about what it is they want students to know, and to examine their work from new perspectives.

▶ *Cross-role* efforts that engage teachers, counsellors, principals and others in learning and professional issues often stimulate shared understanding of goals and practices more effectively than do activities that treat participants as separate groups (Fullan 1991). For example, extended institutes for school-based teams of teachers, administrators and parents have been critical in launching school reforms in Indiana and Kentucky (Lieberman 1995).

We saw the importance of perspective played out similarly in terms of other school routines, such as responsibility for supervising new teachers, course planning, or student assignments. In most settings, these activities were seen as burdens.

However, in some settings they were approached as powerful opportunities for feedback, learning and change; when student teachers were recognized as an important source of new ideas, planning and scheduling were considered occasions for assessment and reconsideration of school or department goals. The extent to which these everyday tasks were considered as learning opportunities depended on the extent to which a culture of inquiry was established at the school.

The critical role of an outsider
Just as individual teachers could not effectively learn alone, learning communities within school require some form of connection to an agent or agency outside the school. Teachers' learning communities successful in enabling teachers' professional growth and positive change in classroom practice were communities with some manner of regular connection to the 'outside' – be it membership in a network, a coach (such as those who work with the Coalition of Essential Schools), a technical assistance team member from a sponsoring project (such as the School Development Project, the Child Development Project and the like), a university colleague or district specialist.

The outsider plays two equally important roles: purveyor of new ideas, and critical friend. A constant theme among teachers working hard to change their practices and rethink their classrooms is that they could not proceed or sustain their efforts without assistance in securing materials, imagining productive classroom activities, and connecting with others knowledgeable about the practices they seek to carry out. 'I have almost more than I can do just to figure out what to do,' said a teacher in a project incorporating new technologies and strategies for students' active participation. 'If I had to get the materials for students to use in their projects, design activities to support each of the computer simulations, think through all of the sequencing, well . . . it just wouldn't happen. I'd go back to what I was doing before, when I was in total control of the classroom.'

Outsiders play an equally essential role in fostering and sustaining 'creative disequilibrium'. Learning communities lacking an outside reality check, critical feedback and coaching can move from shared learning to shared illusions about the group's effectiveness.

Managing school-based communities of practice

These communities of practice and relationships, however, are difficult to manage for multiple reasons. Teachers have little experience or expertise as a 'critical colleague' or member of a learning community. The much remarked-upon isolation of schoolteachers precludes ongoing, substantive discussion about practice; teachers are trained to be 'experts', not learners, to be solo actors not collaborators.

The essential role of an outsider raises other dilemmas. The inevitable dynamic tensions between dependence and independence, insider and outsider are always present. To what extent does an outside coach 'do for' or 'do with'? Experience suggests that 'just in time' assistance is critical to the success of these relationships, as is starting where a teacher group actually is, rather than where the outside agent imagines they are. Technical staff working with the ATLAS project or the Coalition of Essential Schools, for example, find they must often abandon their plans altogether in order to meet teachers where they are. Advancing another agenda, they have learned, almost always frustrates both outsiders and insiders. A difficult task for the outsider is understanding where a teacher community is in terms of norms, expectations and capacity for learning together. A critical first task for an outsider in many settings involves generating an invitation to become involved with a school or teacher community.

Extended communities of practice and opportunities for growth
Important and powerful opportunities for teachers' professional development have been forged outside school, occasions fundamentally different from the district-workshop model of the past. Teachers' professional development in many settings benefited in powerful ways from new arrangements with organizations outside schools:

▶ *School–university collaborations* engaged in curriculum development, change efforts or research. When such relationships emerge as true partnerships, they can create new, more powerful kinds of knowledge about teaching and schooling, as the 'rub between theory and practice' produces more practical, contextualized theory and more theoretically-grounded, broadly informed practice. Educators from schools and universities work together to understand the classroom implications of new ideas, to elaborate concepts, and to share the perspective and expertise particular to their positions (Miller and O'Shea, 1996).
▶ *Teacher-to-teacher and school-to-school networks* that provide 'critical friends' to examine and reflect on teaching and opportunities and to share experiences and efforts to develop new practices. Such networks demonstrate that help helps. They are powerful learning tools because they engage people in collective work on authentic problems that emerge from their own efforts, allowing them to get beyond the dynamics of their own schools and classrooms to encounter other possibilities as well as people who are experiencing and solving similar problems (Lieberman and McLaughlin 1992).

Networks have formed around particular reform strategies, such as the Coalition of Essential Schools; as connections among teachers and schools in a geographic area, such as the Puget Sound Consortium; or around specific topics, such as the California Assessment Collaborative. The oldest and most enduring teacher networks, however, have formed around subject area content. The oldest of these networks, the National Writing Project (NWP), founded in 1974 as the Bay Area Writing Project, has had a profound influence on the teaching of writing in the USA. Since its inception, more than one million educators have participated in NWP projects. NWP and other vital networks operating within and through the American education arena demonstrate that teachers are the best teachers of other teachers, and that successful professional development continues throughout teachers' careers.

▶ *Collaborations between schools and the private sector* help teachers to acquire new expertise in their subject areas, as well as to acquire experience with their students' future workplaces. In California, for example, the Industry Initiatives for Science and Mathematics Education has provided teachers with 763 summer fellowships in more than 70 local businesses and government laboratories, plus $6.5 million and 30,000 volunteer hours for teachers' professional development. Nationwide, an estimated 5500 teachers in 40 states have participated in paid Scientific Work Experience Programmes. These and similar collaborations between schools and the private sector provide teachers with critical information about what the workplace will demand of their students, as well as the opportunity to acquire leading-edge skills and knowledge.

Conclusion: supporting the new professionalism

Rebuilding teachers' professionalism requires 'new wine', or new ideas about the occasions for and the character of teachers' professional development; and 'new bottles', or new structures, opportunities or organizational arrangements to help teachers' efforts to rethink technical culture, classroom expectations for students and professional roles. Supporting teachers' new professionalism assumes a *changed analytical perspective* from which to understand professionalism and professional growth, and a *new theory of practical action* on which to base that support.

A changed analytical perspective

The changed analytical perspective with which to understand teachers' new professionalism has multiple elements. The 'revolution' in cognitive science features the cognitive and conceptual dimensions of learning for both teachers and their students. Routine, expected behaviours move to the background as learner-centred schools subsume traditional rote, fact-driven learning within educational environments that focus on teaching and learning for understanding. The revolution in cognitive science both defines learning outcomes differently and generates new conceptions of teacher and student behaviour that highlight the dynamic, situational character of effective classroom practices.

The new professionalism moves the focus for analysis and action from the individual to the group. The professional communities in which teachers develop new strategies for practice and professionalism are multiple, often only roughly adjacent, and exploit the collective knowledge and understanding of the group. The distributed expertise of the group exceeds and is different from that of any individual (see Lave and Wenger 1991, for example). Teachers' learning communities are 'supra-individual' and cannot be reduced to an aggregation or sum of individuals' attributes, motivations or effects.[5]

This phenomenological perspective highlights social affiliations and opportunities for discourse, rather than individual actions or organizational routines. It shifts attention from rational coordination, contracts and other aspects of bureaucratic organization to interpersonal relationships and ties (see Selznick 1992). In so doing, it provides a powerful way of understanding why the same 'objective realities' – student ethnicity, background academic abilities, for example – can be 'subjectively' and differently interpreted in different contexts (McLaughlin and Talbert 1993). Teachers responded to these 'objective factiticies' (Berger and Luckmann 1967) with reference to the norms, values and ideas about practice that characterize their particular professional communities.

A new theory of practical action

Building a new professionalism for teachers requires new ways of supporting teachers' learning and development. Teachers struggling to respond to the challenges of more rigorous standards of instruction for all students, to change their practices in ways that reflect new ideas about effective teaching and learning, and to adapt to the needs and interests of today's students, find support for their efforts in diverse settings and opportunities. While a coherent policy approach to fostering and sustaining teachers' learning and ongoing professional growth has only begun to be filled out, a number of orienting principles distinguish occasions that are effective in supporting teachers' new professionalism and efforts to reinvent practice. Key principles include:

▶ increasing opportunities for professional dialogue;
▶ reducing teachers' professional isolation;
▶ providing a rich menu of 'nested' opportunities for learning and discourse;
▶ connecting professional development opportunities to meaningful content and change efforts;
▶ creating an environment of professional safety and trust;
▶ restructuring time, space and scale within schools.

These elements of a theory of practical action address reformers' demands that teachers become learners and construct new conceptions of practice and their professional role. This emergent perspective ties professional development directly to teachers' work and to teachers' professional communities. It recognizes the dynamic nature of practice, and the need for capacity-building strategies specific to classroom realities

This new theory of practical action shifts authority within the education system, transferring responsibility for defining, in broad terms, standards for teaching and levelling to professional organizations and projects at the national (or macro) level, while at the same time conferring new authority on teachers and others at the local (or micro) level for specifying the practices and activities appropriate for particular communities, schools and classrooms.

Teachers' multiple and embedded professional communities mediate between macro direction and local enactment of practice. New standards or theories of learning make their way into individual classrooms within and through teachers' professional communities, variously conceived.

A signal feature of this reform era has been the transfer of authority and voice to the profession. In contrast to earlier reform eras where new curricula or assessment strategies were in effect 'handed down' from government bodies, 'experts', publishers or other groups outside the teaching profession, this reform era and the new professionalism it assumes involve teachers in determining what students and teachers should be able to do and know. Professional communities of teachers at national, state, regional and local levels are actively shaping professional outcomes.

With this changed authority comes changed decision-making for many teachers as part of the new professionalism. Teachers now have much more fundamental choices to make about the practices they will carry out in their classrooms – what to do, and how to understand outcomes for students.

Somewhat ironically, and contrary to the fears of those who worried that reforms based on different and more rigorous standards for instruction would usurp teachers' professional autonomy, standards-based reforms can potentially shift authority back to the profession. Indications are that standards-based reforms represented as broad goal statements and not as precise directives for practice have actually enhanced teacher professionalism.

Because they engage teachers in rethinking content, standards-based reforms can also facilitate teachers' acquisition of the pedagogy and perspective consistent with new theories of learning, and construction of practices effective with today's diverse students. By making content problematic, standards-based reforms engender occasion for rethinking all aspects of practice: pedagogy, beliefs about students, and classroom roles. From this perspective, America's reform agenda signals both challenge and opportunity to rebuild teachers' professionalism.

Notes

1 This paper draws from Linda Darling-Hammond and Milbrey W. McLaughlin, 'Policies that support professional development in an era of reform', in M.W. McLaughlin and I. Oberman (eds) (1996) *Professional Development in the Reform Era*. New York: Teachers College Press.

2 Completed or in development are National Standards for Education in the Arts (Consortium of National Arts Education Association); National Standards in Civic Education (Center for Civic Education); National Standards in Economics Education (National Council for Economics Education); National Standards for English Education (National Council of Teachers of English, International Reading Association and the Center for the Study of Reading); (National Standards for Foreign Languages and associations for teachers of French, German, Spanish and Portuguese); National Standards in Geography Education (National Council for Geographic Education); National Standards in History Education (National Center for History in the Schools); Curriculum and Evaluation Standards for School Mathematics, Professional Standards for Teaching Mathematics and Assessment Standards for Mathematics (National Council of Teachers of Mathematics); National Standards for Physical Education (National Association of Sport and Physical Education); National

Science Education Standards (National Research Council); and Curriculum Standards for the Social Studies (National Council for the Social Studies) (Lord 1994: 177–8).

3 Public schooling in America was founded in the early 1800s as an effort to create an educated citizenry on all levels of the new society, a commitment many commentators consider abandoned or at the least eroded at the end of the twentieth century because the educational opportunities available to the nation's schoolchildren are unequal. Ira Katznelson and Margaret Weir offer their book, *Schooling for All*, as a 'memorial to public education as the guardian of a democratic and egalitarian culture in the United States' (1985, p. 8).

4 Proposals submitted under this authority must include a strategy for improving teaching and learning. Activities for in-service education must support:

> the development and implementation of new and improved forms of continuing and sustained professional development opportunities for teachers, principals, and other educators at the school or district level that equip educators with such expertise (necessary for preparing all students to meet standards), and with other knowledge and skills necessary for leading and participating in continuous education improvement.
> [Title III, Section 309 (b) (3) (B)]

5 Taking the group as the most powerful level of analysis replaces functionalist, reductionist analytic frames with perspectives based on social ecology, resource dependence and institutional analysis.

References

Berger, P.L. and Luckmann, T. (1967) *The Social Construction of Reality*. New York: Doubleday.

Bruer, J.T. (1993) *Schools for Thought*. Cambridge, Mass.: MIT Press.

California Center for School Restructuring (1992) *Creating Powerful Learning for All Students: Habits That Help*. San Mateo County Office of Education, California Center for School Restructuring.

Carnegie Forum on Education and the Economy (1986) *A Nation Prepared: Teachers for the 21st Century*. New York: Author.

Case, R. and Bereiter, C. (1984) From behaviourism to cognitive behaviourism to cognitive development: Steps in the evolution of instructional design. *Instructional Science*, 13: 141–58.

Cochran-Smith, M. and Lytle, S.L. (1993) *Inside/Outside: Teacher Research and Knowledge*. New York: Teachers College Press.

Cohen, D.K., McLaughlin, M.W. and Talbert, J.E. (1993) *Teaching for Understanding: Challenges for Policy and Practice*. San Francisco: Jossey-Bass.

Commission on the Skills of the American Workforce (1990) *America's Choice: High Skills or Low Wages!* Rochester, NY: National Center on Education and the Economy.

Damasio, A. (1994) *Descartes' Error: Emotion, Reason and the Human Brain*. New York: GP Putnam and Son.

Darling-Hammond, L. (1993) Reframing the school reform agenda: Developing capacity for school transformation. *Phi Delta Kappan*, 74(10): 752–61.

Etzioni, A. (1969) *The Semi-Professions and Their Organization*. New York: Free Press.

Fullan, M. (1991) *The New Meaning of Educational Change*. New York: Teachers College Press.

Fullan, M. (1993) *Change Forces: Probing the Depths of Educational Reform*. New York: Falmer Press.

Gagne, R.M. (1968) Learning hierarchies. *Educational Psychologist*, 6(4): 2–9.

Gardner, H. (1985) *The Mind's New Science*. New York: Basic Books.

Grossman, P. (1996) Of regularities and reform: Navigating the subject-specific territory of high schools, in M.W. McLaughlin and I. Oberman (eds) *Teacher Learning: New Policies, New Practices*. New York: Teachers College Press.

Jamentz, K. (1996) Assessment as a heuristic for professional practice, in M.W. McLaughlin and I. Oberman (eds) *Teacher Learning: New Policies, New Practices*. New York: Teachers College Press.

Katznelson, I. and Weir, M. (1985) *Schooling for All: Class, Race, and the Decline of the Democratic Ideal*. New York: Basic Books.

Larson, M.S. (1977) *The Rise of Professionalism*. Berkeley: University of California Press.

Lave, J. and Wenger, E. (1991) *Situated Learning: Legitimate Peripheral Participation*. New York: Cambridge University Press.

Lieberman, A. (ed.) (1995) *The Work of Restructuring Schools*. New York: Teachers College Press.

Lieberman, A. and McLaughlin, M.W. (1992) Networks for educational change: Powerful and problematic. *Phi Delta Kappan*, April.

Lieberman, A. and Miller, L. (1991) *Staff Development for Education in the 90's*, 2nd edn. New York: Teachers College Press.

Little, J.W. (1993) Teachers' professional development in a climate of educational reform. *Educational Evaluation and Policy Analysis*, 15(3): 129–51.

Little, J.W. and McLaughlin, M.W. (eds) (1994) *Teachers' Work: Individuals, Colleagues, and Contexts*. New York: Teachers College Press.

Lord, B. (1994) Teacher's professional development: Critical colleagueship and the role of professional community, in N. Conn (ed.) *The Future of Education: Perspectives in National Standards in America*. New York: College Entrance Examination Board.

McLaughlin, M.W. and Oberman, I. (eds) (1996) *Teacher Learning: New Policies, New Practices*. New York: Teachers College Press.

McLaughlin, M.W. and Talbert, J.E. (1993) *Contexts that Matter for Teaching and Learning: Strategic Opportunities for Meeting the Nation's Educational Goals*. Stanford University: Center for Research on the Context of Secondary School Teaching.

Miller, L. and O'Shea, C. (in press) Partnership: Getting broader, getting deeper', in M.W. McLaughlin and I. Oberman (eds) *Professional Development in the Reform Era*. New York: Teachers College Press.

National Commission on Excellence in Education (1983) *A Nation at Risk: The Imperative for Educational Reform*. Washington, D.C.: NCEE.

National Council on Teachers of Mathematics (1991) *Professional Standards for Teaching Mathematics*. Washington, D.C.: NCTM.

Prawat, R. (1992) Teachers' beliefs about teaching and learning: A constructivist perspective. *American Journal of Education*, 100(3): 354–95.

Rogoff, B. (1993) Observing sociocultural activity on three planes: participatory appropriation, guided participation, apprenticeship', in A. Alvarez, P. del Rio and J.V. Wertsch (eds) *Perspectives on Sociocultural Research*. New York: Cambridge University Press.

Selznick, P. (1992) *The Moral Commonwealth*. Berkeley: University of California Press.

Siskin, L.S. (1994) *Realms of Knowledge: Academic Departments in Secondary Schools.* New York: Falmer Press.

Talbert, J.E. and McLaughlin, M. (1994) Teacher professionalism in local school contexts. *American Journal of Education*, 102: 123–53.

Tharp, R.G. and Gallimore, R. (1988) *Rousing Minds to Life: Teaching, Learning and Schooling in Social Context.* Cambridge: Cambridge University Press.

7 JAPANESE LESSONS FOR EDUCATIONAL REFORM

N. Ken Shimahara

Japan's post-war transformation has been remodelled from a nation that burned to ashes in 1945 to one whose annual per capita income is now over $33,000, the highest in the world. That economic transformation measurably epitomizes changes that have occurred in other spheres of Japanese life, although Japanese economic development is not squarely matched by changes in the social and cultural sectors. Japan's economic and social transformation accelerated especially in the 1960s and 1970s, resulting in the rapid globalization of its economy in the succeeding decades. Throughout the post-war era, Japanese transformation has been characterized by a sharp paradox of coexistence of very modern and very traditional attributes. However, because of the fast globalization of its economy, Japan now displays salient characteristics of what other writers have termed *post-modernity*: a 'flexible' economy, information-dominated life, 'internationalization', compression of the boundaries of geographical space, and a shift from a culture of certainty to a culture of uncertainty (Hargreaves 1994).

These forces of transformation are bringing about diversity in a society that has been uniquely uniform. Japan's educational reformers' chief concern in the past decade and a half has been how to diversify its uniform schooling in response to rapid economic and wider social changes. A peculiar and perverse result is that school reform initiatives in Japan on the one hand, and in Britain and the United States on the other, now appear to be moving in opposite directions. Restructuring initiatives in British and American education have placed emphasis on core curriculum, national standards and intensified assessment. It is evident that an increasingly pivotal concern of British and American educational policy has been establishing and enforcing national standards and goals. In contrast, it will be shown that Japanese policymakers are actually seeking to *diversify* their schools. This chapter discusses reform initiatives to diversify high schools in Japan, then analyses the implications for British school reforms. High-school education in Japan is the most critical stage

of schooling in terms of transition to college and employment. High-school education has a striking, lasting impact on adolescents, because the most central part of
that education is preparation for intense university entrance examinations.

Japanese education is now at a crossroads. For more than a decade reformers
have been trying to overhaul it. Today's educational movement began in the early
1980s as a politically initiated, national campaign. Orchestrated deliberations on
school reform gained momentum in 1984 when the national legislature approved
the establishment of the National Council on Educational Reform (NCER). Over
a period of three years NCER issued four reports to recommend a broad range of
change in the school system, based on its findings regarding the state of schooling.
These reports stimulated further reform initiatives in the 1990s. Although reformers'
rhetoric is expected to be bold and far-reaching, the implementation of school
reform is slow and cumulative. This explains why Japan's school reform movement
still continues.

Why are school reforms still urgent in Japan today? Where are they heading?
What implications do they have for reform movements elsewhere? These are the
questions which will be explored in this chapter.

Accomplishments

One of the unique features of Japanese society is that, in very large measure, it
owes its shape to education. As an American anthropologist put it, Japanese society
is 'a meritocracy shaped by an educational competition that enrols nearly everyone'
(Rohlen 1986: 30). Educational credentials and skills are key to employment, social
status and promotion. This accounts for the paramount importance the Japanese attach
to education, and to the demanding entrance examinations for high school and
university. Japanese students' educational achievement, however, is only partially
promoted by the state school system. The infrastructure of education in Japan is
also supported by extensively developed, privately organized schools, existing inde-
pendently outside the standard structure of schooling. These schools, totalling at
least 35,000 throughout the nation (US Department of Education 1987), normally
include *yobiko*, or preparatory schools, and *juku*, which are often categorized into
schools for exam drill, enrichment and remediation. More often than not, parents
also procure private tutorial services to enhance their children's preparation for
entrance examinations. They are usually provided by university students and retired
teachers. All in all, Japan's educational achievement is promoted by a broad societal
and educational infrastructure, of which formal state schooling is just one part.

Much of the ardent interest that the Japanese take in education is rooted in the
development of a meritocratic ethos in the Meiji era of 1868–1912. As Japan
ushered in the era of modernization in the latter half of the nineteenth century, a
revolutionary shift in the pattern of social mobility occurred. The ascribed status
system of the Tokugawa feudal period (1603–1868) was swiftly replaced in the
Meiji era by a system of mobility based on achievement. Part of this modernization

campaign was the development of a comprehensive school system, which was initially laid out as early as 1872, only five years after the Meiji Restoration. By 1890, this system was completed, including the imperial universities.

Drawing upon this historical tradition, and given the wider context of intense interest in educational success within the overall culture, Japan has enjoyed an enviable position both in terms of its unparalleled growth of secondary and higher education in the world, and in terms of its levels of academic achievement. The International Association for the Evaluation of Educational Achievement conducted its first large-scale study in 1964 and a similar one in the early 1980s. Both of these studies tested mathematical knowledge and skills at the eighth and twelfth grade levels, and Japanese students ranked top (Husen 1967; LaPointe *et al.* 1989). The results of the third IAEEA study were reported in November 1996 and this time, Japanese eighth grade students came third in both mathematics and science. Likewise, other studies such as Stevenson and Stigler's (1992) sustained comparative research on elementary student achievement support the high performance of Japanese students. Rohlen (1983) characterized Japanese high school students' knowledge in mathematics and science as equivalent to that of American college graduates.

Problems

Japan has now surpassed the West in some aspects of technological and economic development. The nation was ranked first in the 1993 human development report issued by the United Nations (United Nations Development Programme 1993). The human development index used in this report is a measure of 'human happiness' based on life expectancy, educational standards and individual purchasing power. If Japan's rank in the report is indicative of its advancement, it suggests that the Japanese are now living in a very different social and global context from even two or three decades ago. Even as recently as the 1970s, the nation's development was guided by what has been identified in Japan as a 'catch-up' ideology (Economic Council 1983). Ever since its modernization began in the nineteenth century, Japan's ideology of national development was to catch up with the West in relation to technology, economy and education. Modernization was likened to Westernization, and national development was equivalent to catching up with the West. To accomplish modernization in a much shorter time than the West, Japan developed uniform schooling throughout the nation, controlled by the state, through which it attained high literacy. In the post-World War II period, Japan hardly deviated from this uniform schooling with respect to the curriculum, other school programmes and the control of education, and used this with uniformity to create and supply well-trained human resources.

Now that Japan has indeed caught up with, if not overtaken the West economically, it is seeking a new paradigm of development to replace its 'catch-up' ideology. In the mid 1980s this undertaking was identified as an emerging national concern by Japan's Economic Council, Prime Minister Yasuhiro Nakasone's

Advisory Council on Culture and Education, and others. But in the short term, immediate school reform issues were much more directly related to the effects of uniform schooling and the centrifugal social forces generated by economic affluence and globalization, social mobility, changing family structures, and information-dominated social life. These social forces represented a far-reaching transformation that began in the late 1960s and continued into the early 1980s. Deviant adolescent behaviour including bullying, school violence, refusal to attend school and other forms of juvenile delinquency, dramatically increased in the late 1970s and the 1980s. These frequent incidents of deviant behaviour, which threatened long-standing social norms in Japan, were extensively reported by the mass media and became the subject of a national obsession.

Moreover, overheated high school and university entrance examinations remained a major concern of students, parents and others in society. Entrance examinations had a significant polarizing effect on young people, resulting in the considerable disaffection with schooling of a large proportion of students. As Japan became a 'mature', affluent society, social mobility began to decline, and youths' aspirations for success cooled down remarkably (Amano 1986). By the early 1980s, in other words, Japan's school system, which had been effective in meeting the needs of modernization and industrialization for a whole century, had now become dysfunctional in satisfying the diversified values and needs of youth. Society was becoming diversified but schools were not, creating a lack of fit between the organization of the school system and the pressure of social change. This lack of fit became the principal concern of reformers in the 1980s, and remains so today.

School reforms

In the mid 1980s, the National Council on Educational Reform (NCER) pointed out that Japanese education was suffering from a 'grave state of desolation' caused by pathological conditions in society and schools (NCER 1985). The development of such conditions, in its view, had brought about increasing public criticism and distrust of public education. The Japanese term for desolation is *kohai*, referring to a state of desertedness and deterioration. It was used to make an emotionally charged indictment of schooling. In its First Report, NCER (1985) declared: 'Most important in the educational reform to come is to do away with the uniformity, rigidity, closedness and lack of internationalism, all of which are deep rooted defects of our educational system' (NCER 1985: 26).

Although the reform rhetoric cited here rejected the schooling of Japan's past, what the reforms actually wanted to accomplish was the introduction of some diversity and choice in schooling. A strong theme running through the reform movement in the 1980s was a shared perception that the orientation and structure of Japanese schooling must be altered to meet the exigencies of a much more diverse society, where changes in people's lives resulting from the impact of globalization and the information industry, as well as other influences, were being felt across the nation.

The interest of NCER members in loosening up the nation's school system can be seen especially well in an important debate that focused on the liberalization of schooling. Of the four divisions of NCER, the one that was considering what kind of educational system would be needed for the twenty-first century initially focused on liberalizing the nation's school system in relation to ministry control. The division attributed educational desolation to the uniform schooling that has been maintained by the ministry in the interest of providing equal education throughout the nation. At the outset of its deliberations, this committee concentrated on market-oriented strategies to deregulate schooling, and debated such radical issues as parental freedom to choose any school. This would eliminate the school district system and bring about freedom to establish new schools with little governmental interference, freedom to publish textbooks without the ministry's authorization, the chartering of good *juku* schools, and elimination of the ministry's control over the curriculum (Duke 1986). These ideas were totally unconventional and, if implemented, would have reduced the authority of the ministry to secondary importance (Schoppa 1991).

But proposals for such radical liberalization of Japanese schooling immediately met with outright opposition from the ministry and from the conservative chairman of the NCER division on reforms in elementary and secondary education. Nevertheless, both divisions eventually agreed that the rigid uniformity of Japanese schooling must give way to greater diversity, especially at the secondary level. In this way, diversity rather than liberalization became the dominant theme of reformers' deliberations.

The demand for diversity

Although the continued dominance of uniformity in high school education is still clearly evident today, reformers have considered the need for greater diversity in high school provision from as far back as the 1960s. For example, reformers were instrumental in increasing offerings in vocational high schools in response to the nation's rapid economic and technological advancement in the 1960s (Kurosawa 1994). Nevertheless, their campaign to expand course offerings failed to meet the changing economic and industrial demands of the times, because the fast-changing nature of the demands rendered these programmes obsolete even as they were being developed. As a result, the campaign created little student interest in the new programmes. Instead, it was academic high schools that gained the most popularity as high school enrolment grew rapidly in the 1960s.

The most comprehensive report on educational reform since the Occupation-led reforms of the post-war period emphasized choice and diversity in course offerings within academic high schools. This report was completed in 1971 by the Central Council of Education, an influential advisory body to the Minister of Education. The reforms proposed by the Central Council were ambitious and far-reaching, but their actual impact on the nation's school system was relatively limited, partly because the report did not receive undivided support from the Ministry of Education and national legislators (Schoppa 1991). Top bureaucrats within the ministry who guided the development of Japan's post-war school system stubbornly defended the status quo. Nevertheless, the report offered a fundamental conceptual framework for later school reform initiatives in the 1970s and 1980s, including the reform campaign launched by the NCER.

In brief, the Council recommended that the high school curriculum should be diversified in response to increasing variation in students' ability, aptitude and aspirations. In the context of post-war Japanese high school education, the Council's recommendation was both forward-looking and practical, leading to policy changes at the prefectural (or regional) level in the late 1970s. In response to the Central Council's call for diversity in high school education, the National Association of Prefectural Superintendents began a campaign to consider innovative high school programmes in 1975, which created 'a task force on high school problems' (Kurosawa 1994). In 1977, it issued a report proposing new programmes and 'new types of schools' and in the following year set out detailed plans to transform high-school education. The report was timely because the Ministry of Education also announced a major revision of the course of study for high-school education in the same year. This underscored the creation of greater latitude and relaxation in the construction of school programmes, the humanization of student life, and the promotion of individuality. The new course of study mandated reductions in the number of credits required for graduation and in the number of instructional hours. There were also imaginative strategies to adapt to the greater diversity of students. The Ministry's revised course of study provided the Association with additional legitimacy for its campaign.

The Association's final report contained several important proposals that provided a new direction which fostered the development of innovative high schools. The report proposed broadening course offerings to allow students greater choice and to increase the range of academic programmes. The report also recommended that students be encouraged to take required courses in the sophomore year to allow them to explore their areas of interest in the junior and senior years. Further, it proposed what the Association called 'new types of high schools', which included the following:

► 'credit-based' high schools – schools that would enable students to graduate when they had completed the required credits;
► the clustering of two or three high schools on the same site to coordinate the offering of courses so that students could select courses in a given area of study offered by any cluster school;
► boarding schools – residential schools that would promote all-round education and provide supervision of both the academic and the social aspects of students' lives;
► six-year high schools – schools that would provide effective continuity between middle and high schools.

The recommendations made by the Association eventually became a blueprint for the development of new types of high school. These recommendations resulted in the realization of clustered schools and *sogo sentakusei*, or comprehensive high schools, in various prefectures in the 1980s and 1990s. Nationwide promotion of new types of school, however, required broad public support, financial backing from prefectures across the nation, and, above all, political legitimation. That political legitimation was offered by NCER, whose deliberations on school reforms attracted intense and widespread public attention in the mid 1980s, and by the 1991 reform report of the Central Council of Education.

This latter report included a broad range of recommendations but drew particular attention to the establishment of 'various programmes that synthesize both academic and vocational programmes' (Central Council of Education 1991: 31).

To implement the Council's recommendations, in 1991 the Ministry of Education set up the Committee for the Enhancement of High School Reforms. The Committee (1993) recommended plans to improve high-school education which would involve revamping it to empower students so that they could link their personal interests and future aspirations to formal learning in the school. The Committee's principal recommendation was to implement a comprehensive programme in each high school which aimed to promote students' career aspirations, based on a broad study of both academic and specialized vocational subjects. This comprehensive programme would attract students by offering an alternative to the exclusively college-bound programme. Students who would choose the comprehensive programme would be one of three types: those who are actively interested in linking academic work to career aspirations; those whose primary goal is employment after graduation; and those who have aspirations for college.

The comprehensive programme, it was proposed, would consist of four parts. The first would include the common requirements for all high-school students. The second part would highlight three common areas for students in the comprehensive programme, designated as industrial society and human life, basic studies of information technology, and independent study on selected problems. The third part would consist of rich clusters of elective courses, including: information, industrial management, international cooperation, regional development, biotechnology, welfare management, environmental science, and art and culture. Additional optional studies would make up the fourth part.

Implementation of innovative schools

The current school reform movement finally seems to be giving a new complexion to high-school education. Important, innovative changes are now being introduced piecemeal. First, there are new types of school, whose development precedes the latest campaign to establish comprehensive programmes and has arisen in response to social demands for diversity in upper secondary education. These schools include comprehensive high schools (not comprehensive programmes as later proposed in the 1990s), schools for international studies, schools for information science, and economics and the like. These schools vary in terms of their programmes, the latitude over coursework given to students, and other characteristics. Stimulated by school reform initiatives in the 1980s, the number of innovative schools has been gradually increasing, reflecting enhanced public support for distinctive high schools designed to meet divergent individual and social needs.

Although comprehensive schools are not defined uniformly, schools characterized as comprehensive seem to display common features (Kurosawa 1993). They include: distinctive programmes; a broad selection of courses; encouragement of study in specialized fields from the junior level; an inclusion of both academic and vocational studies; recruitment of students from the entire prefecture, rather than the traditional school districts; an emphasis on foreign languages; competence to process information; international studies; arts (including music and calligraphy); mathematics/science; and the humanities.

Though the development of these schools is still at a relatively early stage, they are expanding throughout the nation, offering alternative formal high-school education to youths. In addition to new types of school, comprehensive programmes have also begun to emerge as a result of the policy initiative by the Central Council of Education. The Committee for Enhancement of High School Reforms (1993) provided conceptual models for these programmes in 1993. The comprehensive programme is now to be developed within given established high schools to provide alternatives for students whose interest cannot be met by distinctly academic or vocational programmes. This programme would meet the needs of a large proportion of students, it has been argued, especially in an academic high school. Although 75 per cent of all the high-school students currently attend *academic* high schools, 30 to 35 per cent of them end up seeking employment, and about 10 per cent of vocational students aspire to college. These students would be a primary target for the comprehensive programme. The Ministry of Education's survey (1993) indicated that six prefectures had already decided to open a comprehensive programme in six high schools in 1994; eight prefectures, in eight schools in 1995. Overall, given the fact that the comprehensive programme is in its initial trial stage, it seems to be off to a good start.

Appraising the reform initiatives

Overall, the initiatives described above illustrate a departure from the traditional academic and vocational curricula in Japanese high schools, and offer promising directions for the future. At present, however, only a small fraction of the nation's 4181 public high schools are participating in these initiatives. One needs to ask, therefore, whether this high school reform movement is a truly committed effort, or faddish. The reform movement in high schools is promising but also modest; yet even this kind of innovation may have limited success in expanding across the system because of certain structural impediments and contrasts within the Japanese system.

First, university entrance examinations remain a perpetual and powerful force that hinders the diversification of high-school education. As confirmed by principals I have interviewed, although innovative schools, especially comprehensive and international schools, offer highly attractive choices to students, the ultimate viability of these schools still depends on how effectively they can prepare students for university entrance examinations. So far these schools have been highly popular, but it is likely that this is only because they have also remained well supported financially.

Secondly, because these schools try to offer unique programmes, such as international studies, they require far more resources than traditional schools. Thirdly, innovative schools also require intrinsic motivation and competence among their teachers to construct a unique curriculum, provide a stimulating teaching approach and offer skilled guidance to pupils. To maintain a positive public image, these schools are expected to meet all these challenges.

Implications for UK educational reform

It is interesting that despite much of the media rhetoric, Japanese and UK school reforms now appear to be evolving in opposite directions. Japan is slowly diversifying its previously standardized schools. England and Wales, meanwhile, have greatly emphasized the criteria of National Curriculum and assessment standards. What reformers in England and Wales are trying to construct, reformers in Japan are in some ways trying to destroy. What the educational experience of post-war Japan reveals is that uniform standards for school programmes fail to address and realize the diverse needs and values of students, which become increasingly precise and acute in the complex, mobile and fast-changing circumstances of post-industrial society. Realizing this problem, Japanese reformers have begun to restructure high schools as a way of expanding students' alternatives. The history of education in Japan, however, suggests that British initiatives to develop national standards in an extensive range of core curriculum subjects at the secondary school level may well have been a mistake, imposing inflexible singular standards on students whose interests and understandings differ greatly because of their membership of a culturally diverse and rapidly changing society (see also Hargreaves 1989; Goodson 1993).

One of the emerging constraints imposed on Japanese and UK schools alike is testing. The national assessment of school achievement has become a policy priority, indeed a virtual obsession, in the UK. The expressed purpose of these national tests has been to measure the extent to which British students have achieved national goals and standards. Although Japan does not employ such tests, its university entrance examinations have served similar purposes by strongly influencing what is taught in high school.

It is clear that national tests in the UK are reinforcing uniformity in the high-school curriculum. As pointed out earlier, what has been seen as the solution in

Britain is ironically one of the greatest problems in Japan, where university entrance examinations have contributed to perpetuating uniformity in instruction at the secondary level. These examinations determine what is considered to be the relevance of the high-school curriculum. In both countries, standardized assessments seem to have a common effect on high-school education: the promotion of uniformity rather than diversity.

In Japan, meanwhile, academic standards at the high-school level are now not nearly such a critical policy issue as the pressing need for diversity. In response to excessive uniformities of the past, and to visible problems of weakened motivation among some Japanese students, Japanese reformers are seriously considering how to make high schools more attractive places for students with different abilities and interests. If it is the standards and the standardization of Japanese and other international models that British policymakers are seeking to emulate in their reform efforts, the models they have selected are discredited models of a uniform past, not models that address a complex and diverse future. The Japanese experience suggests that a critical policy issue for Britain is how to create a more appropriate balance between some common standards and the accommodation of diversity, instead of promoting one at the expense of the other.

References

Amano, I. (1986) The dilemma of Japanese education today. *The Japan Foundation Newsletter*, 13(5): 1–10.

Central Council of Education (1971) Basic policy regarding the reform and expansion of school education, in Koko Kyoiku Henshubu (ed.) (1994) *Primary Documents on High School Education: Reform Reports*. Tokyo: Gakuji Shuppan.

Central Council of Education (1991) *Educational Reforms for a New Age*. Tokyo: Gyosei.

Committee for the Enhancement of High School Reforms (1993) Enhancement of high school education reform. *Monthly Journal of High School Education*, 26(8): 116–54.

Duke, B. (1986) The liberalization of Japanese education. *Comparative Education*, 22: 15–26.

Economic Council (Japan) (1983) *Japan in the Year 2000*. Tokyo: Japan Times.

Furuichi, H. (1994) Interview, 31 May.

Goodson, I. (1993) *Studying Curriculum*. Buckingham: Open University Press.

Hargreaves, A. (1989) *Curriculum and Assessment Reform*. Milton Keynes: Open University Press.

Hargreaves, A. (1994) *Changing Teachers, Changing Times*. London: Cassell.

Husen, T. (1967) *International Study of Achievement in Mathematics*. New York: Wiley.

Kurosawa, Y. (1993) Present status and problems of comprehensive high schools. *Educational Law*, 95: 12–19.

Kurosawa, Y. (1994) What is the aim of high school reforms? *Monthly Journal of High School Education*, 27: 108–13.

LaPointe, A.E., Mead, N.A. and Phillips, G.W. (1989) *A World of Differences: An International Assessment of Mathematics and Science*. Princeton: Educational Testing Service.

Ministry of Education (1993) *Progress Report on Reforms of High School Education.* Tokyo: Ministry of Education.

National Council on Educational Reform (1985) *First Report on Educational Reform.* Tokyo: Government of Japan.

National Council on Educational Reform (1987) *Report on Educational Reform.* Tokyo: Okurasho Insatsukyoku.

Nishimoto, K. (1993) How to create a comprehensive program? *Monthly Journal of High School Education,* 26: 23–9.

Rohlen, T. (1983) *Japan's High Schools.* Berkeley: University of California Press.

Rohlen, T. (1986) Japanese education: If they can do it, should we? *American Scholar,* 55: 29–43.

Schoppa, L. (1991) *Education Reform in Japan: A Case of Immobilist Politics.* New York: Routledge.

Stevenson, H.W. and Stigler, J.W. (1992) *The Learning Gap.* New York: Summit Books.

United Nations Development Programme (1993) *Human Development Report.* New York: Oxford University Press.

US Department of Education (1987) *Japanese Education Today.* Washington, D.C.: US Government Printing Office.

8 FROM REFORM TO RENEWAL: A NEW DEAL FOR A NEW AGE

Andy Hargreaves

Paradoxes of change

In his enigmatically titled bestseller, *The Empty Raincoat*, Charles Handy (1994) remarks that 'paradox has almost become the cliché of our times'. We live in an age of paradox, of forces that simultaneously push and pull us in contradictory directions. As Handy wryly observes, 'sometimes it seems that the more we know, the more confused we get; that the more we increase our technical capacity, the more powerless we become ... We grow more food than we need, but we cannot feed the starving.'

Responding to such paradoxes poses great challenges. But here we are undone by the greatest paradox of all: what Handy calls the paradox of ageing, where 'every generation perceives itself as justifiably different from its predecessor, but plans as if its successor generation will be the same as them'. As we grope towards a better future, our feet are mired in the images and assumptions of our own pasts. This time, says Handy, it needs to be different. We need more informed and imaginative approaches to social change that are not projections of our own generational obsessions. Nowhere is this need for creativity greater than in educational reform.

Consider just five such paradoxes and the challenges they pose for educators:

1 *Many parents have given up responsibility for the very things they want schools to stress.* In Canada, for instance, where I currently live and work, in the same week the public clamoured for 'zero tolerance' policies against violence in schools, *Mortal Kombat* was the top game rental at video stores. And while parents want teachers to get 'back to basics', they continue to allow their children to watch endless television. What parents say they want is not always the same as they themselves encourage.

2 *There is more centralization and more decentralization.* Local management of schools was founded on an ideology of consumer choice, market diversity and

responsiveness to clients' concerns. Meanwhile, the National Curriculum and national attainment tests have brought about greater uniformity and standardization. While the rhetoric has been choice and diversity, the result has been 'Kentucky Fried Schooling'. Schools compete and market themselves mainly as licensed franchises, selling remarkably similar products to their customers.

3 *More globalism creates more tribalism.* This is the paradox of globalization. Economic globalization eliminates borders and imperils national identities. The resulting ethnocentricism has been played out to extremes in places like the Balkans. But packing our National Curriculum with British literature and British history shows that we have been by no means educationally immune from our own ethnocentric panics about nationhood.

4 *More diversity and integration is accompanied by more emphasis on common standards and specialization.* Calls for pupils to have more flexible work skills in the post-industrial economy, and for schools to respond to increasing cultural diversity, are requiring teachers to start looking at their children in terms of multiple intelligences, different learning styles, the development of problem-solving and critical thinking skills, and (in many countries beyond Britain) interdisciplinary links between separate subject domains.

At the same time, obsessions with national strength and identity have spawned standardized tests, international comparisons and competitive league tables of school performance. These sorts of assessment emphasize restricted definitions of intelligence, narrow learning styles, and reaffirmation of subject specialisms that most tests seem to value. We value what we assess instead of assessing what we value. No wonder many teachers are perplexed.

5 *Stronger orientation to the future creates greater nostalgia for the past.* Our nation, like many others, is now one of multiple cultures, values and faiths. Global travel, information and entertainment multiply the contacts between these world views and beliefs even more. Information technology accelerates the pace of scientific learning and also the speed at which we can disconfirm what we have just learned. Morality is now more contested, knowledge more uncertain.

In the face of all this, many people long for golden ages of traditional subjects, basic skills and singular values in a world of moral absolutes and scientific certainties. Some retreat to private schools or to grant-maintained schools that will cherish and protect traditional values. Although, as the late Christopher Lasch (1991) put it, 'nostalgia is the abdication of memory', 'back to the future' still seems to be where many people think schools should go.

How can teachers work with perpetual paradox? How can they be integrated and specialized, standardized and variegated, local and global, inquisitive yet compliant? Sadly, much of the existing literature and practice of educational change offers them only limited help for working with these paradoxes. It advocates brisk and bureaucratic management, when what we need is collective visionary leadership and a new deal for the teachers who will have to make positive change work instead.

Sweeping systemic reforms subject teachers to contradictory mandates, when what teachers need is more flexibility and discretion and higher levels of skills to respond to their children's needs in a complex, paradoxical world. Models and principles of school effectiveness are still peddled which show us how to improve performance in conventional skills and subjects appropriate for the 1960s, but not how to create the kinds of problem-solving and critical thinking that are arguably more necessary in the 1990s (Stoll and Fink 1996). Heroic promises are made to wipe away a few failing schools, but this gives no guidance or stimulus as to how positive change might be achieved in the rest.

Six principles of educational change

Drawing on the analysis of educational change strategies in my recent book *Changing Teachers, Changing Times* (Hargreaves 1994), and on a number of school improvement projects in which I have been and am currently involved, I want to propose six principles of educational change that are more appropriate to our post-modern, post-industrial age. Then I want to close by outlining a 'New Deal' for teachers that I believe could really support them and expect much of them as the vital aspects of positive educational change in the new millennium.

Moving missions

In any change effort, teachers and schools should know where they are going. And broadly speaking, they should be agreed on where they are headed. Purposes matter a lot in teaching. Yet, as Fullan (1993) observes, teachers cannot be *given* a purpose; purposes must come from within. Educational reformers find this hard to accept. Pursuing their own inspiring mission together is what can most help teachers to turn their school around. I have seen this in my own studies of secondary schools making change. The most positive approaches to change were where teachers faced overwhelming challenges in urban schools and were energized by the resolve to work on them together (Hargreaves *et al.* 1992).

Still, we can overdo the 'vision thing'. We can make it stilted and unproductive by locking it up too rigidly in school development plans. These can make the passion of teachers' purposes into a rigid paper formula. Indeed, Wallace's (1991) research has found that teachers often end up writing two development plans – neat, five-year ones that pacify the bureaucrats, and more realistic ones that work for them-selves. As a school principal (headteacher) in the United States said to me within the context of one of my school improvement projects, 'the only thing school develop-ment planning has taught me is how to write better school development plans'.

The other thing about visions and purposes is not to be too single-minded. Common missions that require complete consensus can easily become bland and vacuous because they must appease or appeal to so many different interests. Large secondary schools are particularly prone to this. They are too big and too diverse for everyone to agree. So in conditions of complexity and rapid change, missions will work better if headteachers can live with them being temporary and approximate, and with them not requiring complete consensus. Missions are best thought of as shared journeys, not destinations – always open to revision and review.

Another point about missions, visions and school goals is that they should not just be paper symbols or implicit assumptions that no one ever feels the need to discuss. Goals and purposes should be a vibrant, continuing and explicit part of school life. During a recent visit to schools in Japan, I was struck not just by how the school goals were displayed prominently above the blackboard in each classroom, alongside the class's own goals, but also by how these goals, along with goals for the team that served lunch and the work team of pupils (and teachers!) who cleaned and swept the classrooms and corridors at the end of every day, were all referred to and reviewed explicitly in the ongoing life of the school.

The goals and purposes of these schools are also striking in terms of their imaginativeness and humanitarianism compared with many in Western schools which place more emphasis on individual attainment or self-esteem. Take, for example, the goals of Yodobashi Dairoku Elementary School in Tokyo (in the fractured translation of its own document):

> *Main purpose and policy of the school*
>   *The school puts a great emphasis on the study to educate the pupils who have harmonious and humanistic mind. And bring up the nation who can contribute to the international society.*
>   *The school endeavours to educate to*
> ▶ *A great impression for affairs and phenomenon more seriously*
> ▶ *Reliable comprehension and intentional action*
> ▶ *Responsibility and spirit of peace in international society*
> ▶ *Respect for spirit of independence and positiveness*
> ▶ *Emphasis on the study of international harmony to gain a worldwide perspective.*

Words like 'courage' and phrases that emphasize 'creating children with generous hearts' run through the goals of Japanese schools (Shimahara and Sakai 1995). There are lessons here, perhaps, for how we might revisit, humanize and bring alive the goals and missions of our own schools.

Rekindling the passions of teaching

The theory and practice of educational change need to probe deeper into the heart of what teaching is, and into what moves teachers to do their work well. Good teaching is not just a matter of being efficient, developing competence, mastering technique and possessing the right kind of knowledge. Good teaching also involves emotional work. It is infused with pleasure, passion, creativity, challenge and joy. English primary teachers interviewed by Jennifer Nias (1989) spoke of their relationship to the children in terms of care, affection and even love. But too often educational reform elevates cognition above care as a priority for improvement. Care for persons, things and even ideas, becomes marginalized as a result (Noddings 1992).

In a study of 32 grade 7 and 8 teachers identified as having a serious and sustained commitment to common learning outcomes, integrated curriculum, and alternative forms of assessment and reporting in their classes, we have found that teachers do not plan their courses or units of work in a linear way that starts with the learning they want to achieve, and then identifies the methods and materials which might lead to those outcomes being realized (Hargreaves 1996). Rather, teachers start with knowledge and feelings about their pupils, with their intuitive understanding about what is likely to excite and engage those pupils, and with their own passions and enthusiasms about ideas, topics, materials and methods that they can picture working with their classes. Only after planning collaboratively (and dynamically) with their team colleagues, and sometimes with input from their pupils too, do teachers then go back to the outcomes, as a checklist, to ensure that nothing is out of balance or has been missed out.

Teaching and leading are profoundly emotional activities (Fried 1995). You would not guess this from much of the educational change and reform literature, however. By focusing on knowledge, skill, cognition, decision-making and reflection, those aspects of educational change and teacher development that are rational, calculative, managerial and stereotypically masculine in nature are the ones that are given prominence.

Occupations such as teaching, which involve commitment to the wellbeing of others, involve immense amounts of what Hochschild (1983) calls 'emotional labour'. This emotional labour requires a kind of acting: not just 'acting out' feelings superficially, but also consciously working oneself into experiencing the necessary feelings required to perform one's job well, be these feelings of anger or enthusiasm, calmness or concern. In many respects, this emotional labour is a positive aspect of teaching. Classrooms would be (and sometimes are) barren and boring places without it. But emotional labour also exposes teachers, making them vulnerable when the conditions of and demands on their work make it hard for them to do their emotional work properly.

When teachers are overwhelmed by the demands of change, those who invest themselves emotionally are likely to become racked by guilt, feeling that they are hurting those for whom they care (Hargreaves 1994) Primary teachers trying to cope with the detailed and rapidly-introduced National Curriculum often become crippled by their own conscientiousness (Campbell and Neill 1994), by their determination to make the best of unreasonably imposed demands for the sake of the children they teach. The costs of such intense emotional labour when the conditions of teaching do not support it are that teachers over-extend themselves, burn out, become cynical or leave the profession altogether.

If educational reformers ignore the emotional dimensions of educational change, emotions and feelings will only re-enter the change process by the back door. Festering resentment will undermine and overturn rationally-made decisions; committee work will be poisoned by members with unresolved grudges and grievances;

and pedagogical changes will fail because they have not engaged the passions of the classroom. In the opening chapter, we have already seen how excessively 'clinical' approaches to inspection can wreak emotional havoc of this kind.

Taking our improvement efforts into the emotions of educational change should mean understanding how to create workplaces for teachers that promote positive, even passionate emotional relationships to teaching, learning and improvement. It should also mean protecting teachers from over-extending themselves and from becoming burnt out or cynical as a result. The struggle for positive educational change is one that must involve as many teachers as possible, and that must fully engage their hearts as well as their minds.

Policy realization

If teachers are to review and renew their purposes continuously, they must have sufficient scope to do so. As it is, most educational policy inhibits opportunities for renewal. Its very language of implementation makes teachers mere tools of other people's purposes.

Where possible, policy decisions should be determined at the immediate level where people will have to realize them (Corson 1990). Planned change that follows systematic cycles of development, implementation and review is too inflexible and bureaucratic to respond to local circumstances (Louis 1994). Moreover, detailed documents that freeze policies in text become outdated and are overtaken even as they are being written – by changing communities, new technologies and legislation, and other unanticipated problems (Darling-Hammond 1995).

Creating a continuous and inclusive process of educational policy development and realization is ambitious, difficult and demanding. In the USA, Darling-Hammond (1995) has inquired into 'the kinds of policy supports needed to encourage the participation, learning and risk-taking that are essential for stimulating and sustaining learner-centred teaching and schooling' (p. 18). In many respects, Darling-Hammond argues, 'old paradigm' policy has presented obstacles to, rather than supports for, positive educational change among diverse communities of teachers and learners.

> The tendency of educational policy makers over recent decades has been to assume little knowledge, capacity or ethical commitment on the part of school faculties, and to prescribe practices accordingly – to specify precisely what schools should do and how they should do it. Although many of these prescriptions conflict with one another . . . the top-down approach is comforting to policy makers because it preserves the illusion of control and the pretence of accountability.
>
> [p. 160]

'Old paradigm' policy fails to deal with the problem that 'the complex, contextually different determinants of good practice and of strategies for change cannot be accounted for in the monolithic approach standardized policies require' (p. 160). 'Old paradigm' policy is hierarchical. It lodges design and development responsibility within an administrative elite (with greater or lesser degrees of 'consultation'). It requires teachers to 'implement' (be the tools of) system policies, more than to develop their own. It is a paradigm, Darling-Hammond argues, that has a poor record of educational success. Instead, Darling-Hammond (1995: 160) advises that 'new paradigm' policy

> must find ways to build the capacity of local actors to make good decisions on behalf of their unique students and communities to support their development of knowledge about good practices, their ability to analyze and respond to problems and needs, and their incentives for being collectively responsive and responsible to the children and communities they serve.

The reality of educational policy in almost all areas, Darling-Hammond laments, is that 'menus of reform tactics overwhelm authentic inquiry' among teachers themselves (p. 161). She could well have been writing about the years following the 1988 Education Reform Act in England and Wales. 'New paradigm' policy does not mean administrative indifference or laissez-faire. But it does mean replacing imposed prescriptions for practice with negotiated responsibility for practice – defining new vehicles for accountability that keep everyone's 'eyes on the child, rather than on rules and procedures' (p. 166). In practice, within 'old paradigm' policy:

> When the desired outcomes of hierarchically imposed policies are not realized, policy makers blame the school people responsible for implementation; practitioners blame their inability to devise or pursue better solutions on the constraints of policy. No one can be fully responsible for the results of practice when authority and responsibility are disconnected from one another. When authority is removed from the school, so is accountability for learning. Furthermore, when authority for decision-making is far removed from practitioners and is regulatory in nature, change comes slowly.
>
> [p. 167]

Policy is therefore best established and realized mainly by communities of people within and across schools who talk about the provisions, inquire into them, and reformulate them, bearing in mind the circumstances and the children they know best. This means continuing and even extending some of the current principles of school self-management beyond responsibilities for administration, governance and budget, to the core issues of curriculum itself, and how it might best be matched to the diverse needs of the pupils one teaches.

Reculturing

Before collective action and dialogue can take place, positive relationships must be built among teachers and others, relationships that form the culture of the school. To develop or alter these relationships involves what Michael Fullan and I call reculturing the school (Fullan 1993; Hargreaves 1994).

Among teachers, two kinds of culture have prevailed. In cultures of individualism, teachers have worked largely in isolation, sharing few resources and ideas, and engaging only occasionally in joint planning (Little 1990b). In balkanized cultures, teachers have worked in self-contained sub-groups – like subject departments – that are relatively insulated (Hargreaves and Macmillan 1995). Both cultures fragment relationships, making it hard for teachers to build on one another's expertise. They also stifle the moral support necessary for risk-taking and experimentation. Re-culturing the school to create collaborative cultures among teachers reverses these dynamics. This creates a climate of trust in which teachers can pool resources, take risks, deal with complex and unanticipated problems, support each other through the difficult and dispiriting early stages of learning new teaching strategies, and also celebrate successes.

A key component of reculturing is the wilful involvement of critics and sceptics, who might initially make change efforts more difficult. Building real collaborative cultures means recognizing that dissident views and diverse expertise contribute to effective learning, problem-solving and critical inquiry (Bailey 1995). Constructive reculturing means collaborating with people we do not like as well as people we do (Fullan and Hargreaves 1996). It means valuing mid-career classroom teachers who often feel more comfortable making modest changes with their own classes, as well as valuing young or upwardly-mobile teachers whose commitment to change on a school-wide scale may be more administratively appealing. It means working well with the colleagues we have got, rather than hoping for early retirements and infusions of new blood in their stead.

Restructuring

Cultures do not exist in a vacuum; they are grounded in structures of time and space. These structures shape relationships. Structures of teacher isolation have their roots in schools that have been organized like egg crates since the mid nineteenth century: schools in which children are moved in batches through prescribed curricula, from teacher to teacher, year to year (Hamilton 1989; Goodson 1993). Similarly, balkanized teacher cultures are often a product of subject department structures that go back at least to the Secondary Education Regulations of 1904, and that have been heavily buttressed by the subject-based National Curriculum. Changing cultures to more collaborative forms can also be undermined by existing structures. If the timetable does not allow teachers to meet during the regular school day, for example, collaboration can become exhausting and contrived – tagged on rather than integral to ordinary commitments and working relationships. It is time to change the structural grain, so that teachers can work with it rather than against it.

Some of these structural problems can be solved by administrative ingenuity. Routinely coordinated planning times can bring together teachers who teach the same year or subject. Placing infant and junior teachers in adjacent classrooms can begin to break down stereotypes and boundaries between the different ends of the primary school. In the end, however, it makes no sense to devote so much effort to working around basic structures that are so unsympathetic to professional collaboration.

So that teachers can share problems and information concerning pupils, and not just coordinate key stages and subject matter, we need to look at more pupil-friendly structures that have previously existed in some British schools, and that are now being instituted in the schools of many other countries, such as the USA. Examples of new structures that encourage more collaborative, flexible and responsive ways of working include: teacher teams; multi-age groups; shared decision-making teams; block timetabling; mini-schools or sub-schools, where no teacher meets with more than 80 pupils in a week; and interdisciplinary programmes that bring teachers of different subjects together (Hargreaves *et al.* 1996). The National Curriculum may have improved content and even its coordination and sequencing within the curriculum, but it has often damaged secondary school communities as well: fragmenting teachers' relationships with their pupils and segregating teachers into separate subject factions. Disciplines of content have been tightened, but discipline among pupils has gone the other way. We have had over a decade of redefining subject content. It is time now to rebuild our schools as communities. This is what reculturing and restructuring are about.

Organizational learning

Working together is not just a way of building relationships and collective resolve; it is also a source of learning. It helps people to see problems as things to be solved, not as occasions for blame; to appreciate that conflict is a necessary part of change; to value the different and even dissident voices of more marginal members of the organization; to sort out policy demands; and always to be looking for ways to improve.

Collaborative cultures turn individual learning into shared learning. Attending to structures so they help people to connect, and designing tasks so they increase our capacity and opportunities for learning, spreads such learning across the entire organization. This is what Peter Senge, in his book *The Fifth Discipline*, means by 'organizational learning' (Senge 1990). Learning organizations, he says, are: 'Organizations where people continually expand their capacity to create the results they truly desire, where new and expansive patterns of thinking are nurtured, where collective aspiration is set free and where people are continually learning how to learn together.'

Schools that are good places for children's learning must be good places for teachers' learning also (Sarason 1990). As my colleague Michael Fullan (1993) has said, too many schools are not now learning organizations. We need to build into the system more time and incentives for professional learning, to create more opportunities for teachers to connect with each other in the classroom as well as in the staffroom, and to foster the kind of visionary leadership that includes staff collaboratively in the change process instead of imposing changes managerially upon them. Climates in which teachers are blamed for every educational failure, and shamed into putting them right, are absolutely contrary to every principle of organizational learning. A learning society must be one where policymakers learn from its teachers, and where they promote professional learning among teachers themselves. A New Deal for teachers must be one in which there is no longer any advantage in (or need for) embellishing one's successes and disguising mistakes when the inspector calls; and in which teachers no longer gain any benefit from hiding good ideas from their colleagues in neighbouring schools so that they can maintain an edge over them in the competition for clients.

A New Deal for teachers

Bureaucratic management, burdens of imposed content and assessments, and market orientations that divide schools and teachers from one another, have created poor conditions for organizational learning, or for effective educational change of any kind. Other change strategies are possible. Some schools already practise them. Teachers have endured years of educational reform imposed from without. It is now time to look at ways of stimulating and supporting learning and renewal among teachers from within. Moving from reform to renewal seems the most promising and the most professional path that government strategies in education can now take at the turn of the century. What, specifically, might this mean?

Teaching with passion, renewing one's basic purposes as a teacher, knowing how to use power with others to benefit the children you teach, committing to structures of work and timetabling that put children's needs before your own routines and securities – these are some of the basic principles of what it means to teach successfully in an age of paradox. But teachers cannot do all this by themselves. Hope, spirit and individual effort mean a lot, but the conditions need to be right for these things to spread beyond a few heroic individuals so that whole groups of teachers can be galvanized into meeting the challenges of the postmodern age. So I would like to close by outlining six directions that policymakers might usefully pursue at the end of the century if they really want to move beyond trying to change teachers in this way or that way, and instead create the conditions, supports and climate of expectation that will enable and encourage teachers to change themselves. These six directions all spring from analyses that have been undertaken at different points in this book. They also point to a scenario in which actions are moved by the belief that, just as children perform better when we expect a lot of them and when we give them the skills and supports they need to achieve (and not when we humiliate them, show them up, or make them feel recalcitrant failures), so too are we likely to raise the standards of teaching if we expect that teachers really can do this themselves, if we give them the necessary supports to achieve this goal, and if we remove the bureaucratic annoyances, impositions and interferences that get in their way. These directions, I believe, could form part of a significant New Deal for teachers in which they become agents rather than objects of educational change – change that in the end only they can bring to fruition with the pupils that they teach.

A self-regulating profession

The teaching profession must become, and be allowed to be, self-regulating. This self-regulation must not be symbolic or tediously bureaucratic. It must be rigorous and robust – getting to the heart of what good quality teaching and learning is all about. A self-regulating profession must set, maintain and constantly look for ways to raise its own standards of practice, rather than having other people's standards imposed upon its members. This could be achieved by establishing a General Teaching Council (GTC). All teachers in state schools should be required to be members of this Council. Private schools, as ever, may want to employ unlicensed teachers, and that will be their own choice, but informed clients will surely not overlook any school's apparent indifference to standards that have been set by the wider profession. The General Teaching Council's controlling body should be numerically dominated by teachers elected by their fellow colleagues. Existing officials or representatives of teachers' unions or of teachers' employers (such as LEAs) should not be allowed to stand for election. The Council must be, and be seen to be, absolutely independent of unions and employers, and not be caught up in conflicts of interest. The Council's controlling body should also include appointed and co-opted members from the wider community such as parents, employers, trade unions, governors, universities, faculties of education, minority communities and so on. The actions of this controlling body of the GTC should be accountable and transparent.

Like other General Teaching Councils, such as those in Scotland or in British Columbia, Canada, the Council should control issues of registering and licensing teachers; it should set up and apply codes of professional ethics; and it should discipline its members for misconduct or incompetence where necessary. But for the GTC to be a truly rigorous body of self-regulation, its responsibilities must extend much more widely than this. It should:

▶ establish and apply standards of professional practice;
▶ create a national framework of criteria, expectations and requirements for professional learning;
▶ work collaboratively with Government to create educational policies that support and do not interfere with successful professional learning;
▶ work collaboratively with Government to create a national framework of certification and ongoing professional learning for headteachers;
▶ work collaboratively with universities and other higher education institutions to accredit programmes of initial teacher education;
▶ accredit providers of in-service teacher education.

A body such as this would put teachers in the forefront of standards-setting. It would give voice to all sectors of the profession. It would act as a powerful pressure group on Government to create policies that promote the high standards of practice and professional learning which teachers would have set themselves. It would give teachers the privilege and the responsibility of establishing their own collective professionalism, so they are truly champions of educational reform.

A continuous record of learning

Teachers have a right to high-quality professional learning experiences and opportunities. They also have a responsibility to be always on the look-out for ways to teach and reach their pupils more effectively. Teachers who see teaching as something that is basically easy, something that is mastered in early career and that they then know how to do for the rest of their life, get poorer results than teachers who see teaching as being intrinsically difficult, something in which improvement is always possible and necessary (Rosenholtz 1989). Pupils become good learners when they are in the classes of teachers who are good learners. Professional learning for teachers should therefore not be seen by teachers, schools or Governments as peripheral to their priorities. Teachers, more than anyone, are essential to the creation of a new learning society. They can scarcely help to create such a society if they are not good learners themselves.

Schoolteaching is no job for amateurs. In what I have elsewhere called the pre-professional age of teaching, the technical aspects of the job were uncomplicated and unquestioned (Hargreaves 1997). Teachers were (at best) enthusiastic people who knew their stuff, knew how to get it across and could keep order in their classes. You learned to teach by watching others do it, first as a pupil, then as a student teacher. After that, barring a few refinements gained through trial and error, you knew how to teach and you were on your own. Although teaching has changed dramatically in recent years, these pre-professional archetypes of teaching remain pervasive in our culture (Sugrue 1996; Weber and Mitchell 1996). The teachers who taught us and who taught those who make policy for teachers now, were usually teachers who belonged to this pre-professional age. Pre-professional images therefore continue to influence many policymakers' understandings of what teaching is. This is one reason why the case for more and better professional learning in teaching is so hard to make. If the task of teaching is basically simple, why do we need to invest in continuous professional learning, beyond a few in-service training sessions connected to the Government's latest policies?

For teachers and policymakers alike, it is time to come to terms with the fact that in a technologically complex and culturally diverse society where children have many different ways of learning, teaching is inherently very difficult, and becoming more and more difficult by the day. Professional learning can therefore no longer be an optional luxury for course-going individuals, nor a set of add-on workshops to implement Government priorities. Professional learning must be made integral to the task of teaching, to dealing effectively with the numerous new challenges that teachers face in their work, and to getting better as a teacher over time. In the complex, rapidly changing post-modern age, if you do not get better as a teacher over time, you do not merely stay the same: you get worse.

So how do we create stronger commitments to continuous professional learning? One strategy, previously outlined in Day's chapter, is for every teacher to have a plan or portfolio of continuous professional learning. Having a portfolio, of course, necessitates having professional learning experiences to put in it. And this will surely exert pressure on some teachers to think more reflectively about their teaching, what they want to improve in their teaching, and how they want to set about doing that. Yet this process could also be designed to give every teacher the right to discuss his or her own professional learning and associated career plans with a colleague or mentor on a periodic basis – and to receive good-quality feedback, advice and support that many teachers do not now get. Moreover, professional learning plans provoke a demand for professional learning provision – not just in terms of courses, but in terms of time and resources as well. Too many teachers are starved of good-quality professional learning because managers or policymakers have insufficient commitment to providing it. The cumulative effect of professional learning planning will be to put pressure on such people to meet their obligations for provision.

Lastly, professional learning portfolios can also act as instruments of accountability if they are in whole or in part submitted to a self-regulating General Teaching Council on a periodic basis. This will enable the Council to keep track of overall professional learning patterns, to put pressure on providers to meet their professional learning obligations, and to call to account any individuals whose professional learning portfolio contents appear to be scant or missing. This seeming shortfall in professional learning may signal serious problems in individual teachers' commitments to professional learning; it may point to mitigating circumstances in a teacher's career demands or life circumstances; it may reveal poor management which does not value the teacher's professional learning or makes few opportunities available for it; or it may unearth a whole store of valuable experiences which the teacher concerned had not considered to be worthwhile professional learning at all. What matters here, in terms of the General Teaching Council's involvement, is that professional learning is systematically encouraged, that it is transparently accountable, and that where it gives cause for concern, it is also actionable.

In all this, it is important to recognize that professional learning means more than collecting courses and certificates. Nothing could be worse than that the requirement for a professional learning portfolio should propel teachers into a cynical chase for pieces of paper. Any framework for or process of professional learning must take into account the extensive research on successful professional learning (e.g. Little 1993). In this, certificated courses, inspirational speeches and isolated workshops are normally much less effective than professional learning which is at some point built into teachers' everyday working responsibilities. Professional learning is usually most successful when:

▶ teachers pursue it collaboratively, rather than individually;
▶ it addresses questions that are compelling for teachers, not concerns imposed by others;
▶ it is connected (but not necessarily restricted) to the ongoing priorities of the school;
▶ commitment to it is long-term and sustained, not short-term and episodic.

What this means is that the kinds of professional learning that can and should be documented and encouraged through professional learning portfolios should include things like starting a team-teaching relationship, being a 'critical friend' for a colleague, planning an interdisciplinary unit of work with another department, writing a textbook, being a mentor for a new teacher, collecting data from pupils about your courses and making adjustments because of them, and so forth. Processes of the kind I have described do not only *record* teachers' professional learning, they also stimulate and renew it.

Strong professional communities

Even where professional learning is embedded in school priorities and teachers' classroom practices, and is not undertaken in isolation but with other colleagues as a team, if teachers in the school are not routinely used to working together, trusting each other, and providing mutual support, specific professional learning initiatives are likely to fail. Research consistently shows that mentor systems or peer coaching relationships among teachers tend to be more effective where giving and receiving help are already accepted and valued practices among teachers in the school as a whole (Little 1990). Otherwise, getting help is seen as a sign of weakness, mentor relationships deviate dramatically from the norm, and new teachers want to escape from them as fast as they can. Similarly, school development planning can be stilted, and curriculum coordination contrived, if it is tacked onto professional cultures in which teaching is seen as easy, support as unnecessary and isolation as the norm. Teams thrown together to complete specific tasks can dispatch managerial obligations adequately enough (Webb and Vulliamy 1996), but only strong, ongoing cultures of collaboration can elevate standards of practice and sustain continuous professional learning (Nias 1989; Hargreaves 1994).

High-quality professionalism, then, is not just an issue for a representative body such as a General Teaching Council, but also for every school or department as its own local professional community. Building strong teacher cultures, or what McLaughlin in her chapter called strong, local professional communities, leads to better teacher learning and with it, better pupil learning (Rosenholtz 1989). This is because strong professional communities:

▶ promote risk-taking and willingness to experiment with new teaching strategies among teachers;
▶ create higher senses of efficacy among teachers, who feel more able to make a difference for pupils;
▶ encourage commitment to continuous learning and improvement in an occupation that is seen as inherently difficult;
▶ build consistency of expectations for pupil learning and behaviour that are embedded in teachers' day-to-day understandings and behaviour, and not just in paper policies and procedures;
▶ foster and value norms of collaboration, mutual support and reciprocal help-giving that improve the school's capacities for problem-solving;
▶ see pupil problems as things that teachers can solve together, not as things to tell stories about or things to blame on teachers' own ineffectiveness.

Making schools into strong professional communities is one of the most urgent and difficult tasks for bringing about substantial and successful educational change in the new century. It means governments and management coming to see educational change not as a process where teachers will fearfully comply with external requirements, but as one that teachers work on together, in communities of practice, where they talk about teaching together, discuss new strategies (and not just particular lesson plans), are always open to new ideas, exchange and talk about professional reading, observe and give feedback on each others' teaching, and so on. As I argued earlier, it means acknowledging that most school problems present themselves in unique circumstances and combinations and are best solved by informed local professional judgement, not by standardized procedures or solutions. Making schools into communities where teachers talk about teaching, think about teaching, collect and analyse data on the effects of their teaching, look at other people's teaching, and are always searching for ways to improve their own teaching, will raise standards much more quickly than forcing teachers' compliance with requirements imposed from the outside.

But building strong professional communities in many schools, not just a few, means that Governments and management must get a real grip on how to change schools as organizations. Schools need to have a clear structure that fosters learning for their teachers, just as much as they need structures that foster learning among their pupils. One of the trickiest problems in this respect is time. Time for teachers to meet and reflect during the school day is essential to creating strong professional communities. One of the greatest struggles in the future of teaching should not be so much about the size of classes teachers teach (though this is also an important issue), but about the amount of time teachers have away from those classes – to undertake planning, reflection and observation with colleagues so as to improve the quality of their teaching in the long term. There is no positive change without time to understand it and undertake it. Absence of time isolates teachers from their colleagues when they most need to be alongside them – in teaching situations as well as talking and planning ones. And isolation, we have seen, keeps quality low. A New Deal for teachers must include terms and conditions of work that are built on different assumptions about time and its distribution, where teachers work a little more with colleagues and a little less in classrooms than they have done in the past. Such a policy is not an extravagant indulgence. On the contrary, improvements in quality of what goes on inside the classroom are highly dependent on improvements in what goes on outside it (Fullan and Hargreaves 1996). Teacher time is one of the nettles that Government must now grasp.

Strong professional communities also prosper from excellent leadership which really motivates people, and does not merely manage them. Leadership training programmes must select, license and develop headteachers who can build good morale; motivate staff to excel; promote learning, inquiry and problem-solving; value people for their efforts; be able to give critical feedback in constructive ways; and tinker creatively with structures and resources so as to strengthen opportunities for collaboration and the ability of the community to learn. As it is with corporations, so it must be with schools; leadership for line management in cultures of compliance must give way to leadership for learning in cultures of change.

Inspection plus review

Hard-headed external inspection is often seen as the antithesis of self-evaluation and internal review. Inspection is seen to be tough, fair, objective and accountable. Self-evaluation and review are not.

External inspectors can look at schools with fresh eyes, put them in perspective by comparing them with schools elsewhere, and (in the shape of Ofsted, at any rate) make judgements that matter for what happens next. By comparison, internal review can be restricted by the experiences of those who perform it, have limited comparability with schools elsewhere, and be too inclined to gild the lily in the final report. In addition to all this, self-evaluation can be exhausting and time-consuming for those who undertake it.

Yet in the first chapter particularly, we have seen how Ofsted inspections can wreak emotional havoc on those who are exposed to them. They can clinically expose weaknesses while offering no support for remedying them. In print at least, they amount to monologues of non-negotiable judgement rather than dialogues of constructive learning and critique. At the same time, while the products of self-evaluation can be cosmetic and compromised, the self-evaluation process is often much more ruthlessly self-searching than a passing external inspection can ever really be. Getting teachers to gather and analyse data about their own practice and its consequences, can disturb their assumptions and complacency much more than unwanted external judgements usually can.

External inspection and internal evaluation each have their strengths and weaknesses. The choices that policymakers make between them are usually based on ideology, values and prejudice rather than on a rational appraisal of their respective merits – just the kind of accusation that these selfsame policymakers often make about the way classroom teachers usually justify *their* pedagogical choices, in fact. But the two processes need not be mutually exclusive. It is not necessary to decide between them; they can be brought together in highly productive ways.

In parts of Australia, and previously in parts of England too, reviewing the performance of a school and its teachers has sometimes been built on two evaluations – a self-evaluation undertaken by teachers and others within the school, and an evaluation performed by people with fresh eyes who come from outside it. The final report results from dialogue between insiders and outsiders, between people who know what it is really like to be in this special place and people who have a clearer sense of how things can be different elsewhere.

What matters most is the quality of learning that can occur when insiders and outsiders review the quality of the school's performance together. Insiders learn from asking their own questions, gathering disturbing data and having to confront, talk about and act upon the gaps between what they thought they were achieving and what they were actually achieving. Secondly, they also learn from what the outsiders see and say about their practice. Just as visitors to our country can help us see ourselves anew through their inquisitive and uncomprehending eyes, so the outside inspector's advantage is to be able to make teachers look at themselves again, no matter how uncomfortable that might be. Equally, courageous teachers working in difficult communities, who may have become dispirited by seemingly insurmountable obstacles, or by having achieved only modest steps to success, can have their hopes lifted by external inspections which can testify to just how much they are achieving compared with colleagues and communities elsewhere. Lastly, teachers learn a lot from the dialogue between insider and outsider as each struggles to understand the other's point of view and to articulate their own.

Effective school evaluation involves both judging and learning. But the judging has become too one-sided, and professional learning has suffered as a result. This does not mean that inspection should be abolished; but it should be reinvented as a process that is carried out in partnership with schools, as a process that is more transparent to those who are exposed to it, and as a process that, where it points to difficulties and weaknesses, has direct links to support systems which can remedy them.

Teacher research

One reason why external inspection or even self-evaluation are so traumatic for many teachers is the amount of time and energy teachers must devote to gathering data or compiling documentation for when the inspector calls or the review is due. Teachers do not normally gather data, still less analyse them as a routine part of their work. So when the moment for inspection comes, herculean efforts must be diverted into putting together all the necessary paperwork. This is not only daunting to teachers and a huge drain on their time and energy, but it is also experienced as a damaging distraction from what teachers consider most important – teaching itself.

Yet if data gathering and analysis went on all the time, as a routine part of what teachers did, most of the documented evidence would already be in place when the inspector's visit was announced, and the effort needed to pull it together would be much less extreme. So why do so few schools gather, sort and analyse data in the ordinary course of their work – not just data on achievement and attendance, but also on changes in teachers' practices, pupils' responses to school, the take-up and impact of new teaching strategies and so on?

One reason is that many teachers prefer doing things to pausing and reflecting about them. Doing things – inventing, improvising, adapting – is what the hurly-burly or immediacy of classroom life constantly demands (Jackson 1988). There is not really time to step back much, and when eventually there is, you may find you do not even want to any more. A new lesson, a new activity, a better wall display may give you more of an immediate buzz than a painstaking evaluation of just how well the last set of strategies went.

But time is as serious a problem as inclination. Gathering data and analysing them is demanding, sustained and focused work. Research cannot be squeezed into a few spare moments or undertaken off-the-cuff. Not every teacher wants to be, is cut out to be, or has the time to be a researcher (Hammersley 1993). But schools would really benefit greatly from undertaking their own ongoing research: as a source of professional learning, and as preparation for moments of inspection and review.

Because teacher research is needed but not every teacher can do it or wants to, I therefore propose that every medium-sized secondary school or above should have its own teacher leadership position with responsibility for research (smaller schools can share a teacher leader of this kind). The responsibilities of such teacher leaders would include:

▶ collecting and interpreting readily available data on the composition of the student body and outcome data on achievement, attendance, suspensions, expulsions etc.; data on the age and career profiles of staff, etc.;
▶ coordinating the technical aspects of school documentation at times of inspection and review;
▶ undertaking a needs assessment or gap analysis whenever the school embarks on a major initiative;
▶ searching out existing evidence related to any proposed initiative the school is undertaking, e.g. a new system of ability grouping, the use of cooperative learning strategies, etc.;
▶ mediating published research to the school staff by responding to staff requests, placing relevant reports in staff pigeonholes, etc.;
▶ stimulating and coordinating classroom action research between individuals or small groups of teachers;
▶ helping to publicize the results and processes of school-based research to the wider professional community.

Professional learning support

Not all successful professional learning is school-based. Teachers have a lot to learn from colleagues in other schools as well as their own. The well of experience on which any one school staff draws will eventually run dry. But the need to talk to other teachers has not always been well served by the market system of parental choice. Neighbouring schools that compete for clients are unlikely to share their expertise. And professional development providers have become just as subject to the market as individual schools. So professional development provision has become an uneven mosaic of universities, LEAs, private consortia, independent consultants and of schools that help themselves. Some of this provision is excellent; some of it very hit-and-miss. As we saw in Chapter 1, this provision has, if anything, tended to be available more to managers than to the managed. Chapter 1 described the vacuum that had opened up in professional development, where greater choice also seemed to mean less professional community. How might this vacuum now be filled?

While professional learning standards and criteria should be a national responsibility, professional learning provision is best coordinated regionally. I therefore propose the establishment of a network of regional professional learning agencies, larger than single local education authorities, whose overall purpose would be to establish some coherence of professional learning activity and to build a wider sense of professional community among teachers undertaking professional learning. Specifically, regional professional learning agencies (RPLAs) would:

► *advise individual schools on professional learning needs and provision.* RPLAs could be particularly helpful in connecting the schools to relevant consultants and providers, and also in helping schools to see the value of professional learning that extends beyond courses and certificates, so they might use professional learning resources to help teachers visit other schools, spend time in one another's classes, bring other adults into the school, and so forth;

► *bring schools together which are engaged in similar initiatives* so that their staffs can engage in shared learning, mutual school visits, pooled resourcing for hiring external consultants, etc. In market systems of parental choice, RPLAs could be especially helpful in bringing together schools which are not in geographical proximity to, and therefore not in direct competition with, one another;

► *serve as a clearing house for accredited professional learning providers*, by publishing their services in a clearly written guide;

► *assist schools and their teacher-research leaders to prepare for inspection and undertake reviews;*

► *establish one or more teachers' centres*, run and staffed by teachers as shared communities of professional learning to which teachers from all schools would belong, and where they could meet with colleagues, access resources and undertake courses as they saw fit;

► *initiate and support computer networks of professional learning* among teachers within and beyond the region, where teachers can discuss problems, seek advice, relay gossip, exchange lesson plans, suggest professional reading, etc.

Conclusion

These six broad directions through which teachers can be brought back into the educational reform process have given rise to seven specific proposals and recommendations that would make up a much-needed New Deal for teachers. To summarize, and to close, these are:

1 *Create a self-regulating General Teaching Council*, controlled by an elected majority of teachers, which will be independent of unions and employers, and will control teacher licensing and registration, define and apply codes of professional ethics, discipline its members where appropriate, establish and apply standards of professional practice, create a national framework for professional learning, work with Government to ensure policy initiatives support teachers' professional learning,

work with higher education to accredit programmes of initial teacher education, and accredit providers of in-service teacher education.

2 *Establish a universal system of professional learning portfolios* for teachers in state schools, to stimulate and monitor continuous professional learning for all.

3 *Make time for professional learning and dialogue within the school day,* a key resourcing issue for schools, a central bargaining point for unions, and a key policy priority for Government so that schools can become strong professional learning communities.

4 *Establish national training programmes in educational leadership in which abil-ity* of present or intending headteachers *to create and sustain strong professional learning communities* in their schools *is counted as a key competence* or essential criterion of certification and success.

5 *Redesign present inspection processes* to become a combination of, and dialogue between, external inspection and internal review.

6 *Assign one teacher leadership position in teacher research to every middle-sized secondary school or above,* or to groups of schools that are smaller in size.

7 *Create a network of regional professional learning agencies* (RPLAs) to advise individual schools on their professional learning needs and how best to meet them, to bring staff together who are engaged in similar initiatives, to be clearing-houses for accredited professional learning providers, to help schools prepare for inspections and reviews, to establish local teachers' centres, and to support computer networks of professional learning.

References

Bailey, B. (1995) Teachers marginalized by mandated change. Unpublished PhD thesis. Toronto: Ontario Institute for Studies in Education.

Campbell, R.J. and Neill, S.R. (1994) *Primary Teachers at Work*. London: Routledge.

Cooper, C. (1994) *Guardian*, 18 November.

Corson, D. (1990) *Language Policy Across the Curriculum*. Clevedon, Avon: Multilingual Matters.

Darling-Hammond, L. (1995) Policy for restructuring, in A. Lieberman. *The Work of Re-structuring Schools*. New York: Teachers College Press.

Fried, R. (1995) *The Passionate Teacher*. Boston: Beacon Press.

Fullan, M. (1993) *Change Forces: Probing the Depth of Educational Reform*. New York: Falmer Press.

Fullan, M. and Hargreaves, A. (1996) *What's Worth Fighting for in Your School?*, 2nd edn. New York: Teachers College Press.

Goodson, I. (1993) *Studying Curriculum*. Buckingham: Open University Press.

Hamilton, D. (1989) *Towards a Theory of Schooling*. New York: Falmer Press.

Hammersley, M. (1993) On the teacher as researcher. *Educational Action Research*, 1(3): 425–45.

Handy, C. (1994) *The Empty Raincoat*. Cambridge, Mass.: Harvard Business Press.

Hargreaves, A. (1994) *Changing Teachers, Changing Times: Teacher's Work and Culture in the Postmodern Age*. London: Cassell.

Hargreaves, A. (1997) Rethinking educational change, in A. Hargreaves *Rethinking Educational Change with Heart and Mind: The 1997 ASCD Yearbook*. Alexandria, VA: Association for Supervision and Curriculum Development.

Hargreaves, A. and Macmillan, R. (1995) The balkanization of teaching (with R. Macmillan), in J.W. Little and L.S. Siskin (eds) *Subjects in Question*. New York: Teachers College Press.

Hargreaves, A., Davis, J., Fullan, M. *et al.* (1992) *Secondary School Work Cultures and Educational Change*. Toronto: Ontario Institute for Studies in Education.

Hargreaves, A., Earl, L. and Ryan, J. (1996) *Schooling for Change*. New York: Falmer Press.

Hochschild, A. (1983) *The Managed Heart*. Berkeley, Calif.: University of California Press.

Jackson, P. (1988) *The Practice of Teaching*. New York: Teachers College Press.

Lasch, C. (1991) *The True and Only Heaven: Progress and its Critics*. New York: W.W. Norton.

Little, W.J. (1990a) The mentoring phenomenon and the social organisation of teaching. *Review of Research in Education*, 15.

Little, W.J. (1990b) The persistence of privacy: Autonomy and initiative in teachers' professional relations. *Teachers' College Record*, 91(4): 509–36.

Little, W.J. (1993) Teachers' professional development in a climate of educational reform. *Educational Evaluation on Policy Analysis*, 15(2): 129–51.

Louis, K.S. (1994) Beyond managed change: Rethinking how schools improve. *School Effectiveness and Improvement*, 5(1): 2–24.

Nias, J. (1989), *Primary Teachers Talking*. London: Routledge and Kegan Paul.

Noddings, N. (1992) *The Challenge to Care in Schools*. New York: Teachers College Press.

Rosenholtz, S. (1989) *Teachers' Workplace*. New York: Longman.

Sarason, S. (1990) *The Predictable Failure of Educational Reform*. San Francisco: Jossey-Bass.

Senge, P. (1990) *The Fifth Discipline: The Art and Practice of the Learning Organization*. New York: Doubleday.

Shimahara, K. and Sakai, A. (1995) *Learning to Teach in Two Cultures*. New York: Garland Publishing.

Stoll, L. and Fink, D. (1996) *Changing Our Schools*. Buckingham: Open University Press.

Sugrue, C. (1996) Student teachers' lay theories: Implications for professional development, in I. Goodson and A. Hargreaves (eds) *Teachers' Professional Lives*. London and New York: Falmer Press.

Wallace, M. (1991) Contradictory interests in policy implementation: The case of LEA development plans for schools. *Journal of Education Policy*, 6(4): 385–99.

Webb, R. and Vulliamy, G. (1996) *Roles and Responsibilities in the Primary School: Changing Demands, Changing Practices*. Buckingham: Open University Press.

Weber, A. and Mitchell, C. (1996) Using drawings to interrogate professional identity and the popular culture of teaching, in I. Goodson and A. Hargreaves (eds) *Teachers' Professional Lives*. London and New York: Falmer Press.

INDEX

WHAT'S WORTH FIGHTING FOR IN YOUR SCHOOL?
WORKING TOGETHER FOR IMPROVEMENT

Michael Fullan and Andy Hargreaves

This is about how to make schools more interesting and fulfilling places to be. It tackles how to bring about marked improvements in the daily lives and experiences of teachers, heads and pupils. The premise is that teachers and heads themselves should ultimately *make* this happen.

Almost everywhere, teachers and heads are overloaded and undervalued. Teachers and heads will need to take more of the initiative themselves, not just in holding off unreasonable demands, not just in bargaining for better conditions but also in making constructive improvements of their own, as a professional community. Examples of such constructive practice already exist but they need to be broadened, strengthened and developed. This book is meant to stimulate such improvements. It is a practical book and a provocative one; fully aware of the constraints and everyday problems facing teachers but clear in setting out what really is worth fighting for in schools.

No teacher or head will read this book without responding in the light of his or her personal experiences, beliefs and passion about teaching; and all will be challenged by this catalyst for action.

Contents
Preface to the British edition – Foreword – Acknowledgements – The authors – Introduction – The problem – Total teachers – Total schools – Guidelines for action – References.

160pp   0 335 15755 6 (paperback)